God
of
Both

Landon McGarry

God of Both

Trilogy Christian Publishers A Wholly Owned Subsidiary of Trinity Broadcasting Network

2442 Michelle Drive Tustin, CA 92780

Rights Department, 2442 Michelle Drive, Tustin, CA 92780.

Trilogy Christian Publishing/TBN and colophon are trademarks of Trinity Broadcasting Network.

Cover design by: Steven Cipres

For information about special discounts for bulk purchases, please contact Trilogy Christian Publishing.

Manufactured in the United States of America

10 9 8 7 6 5 4 3 2 1

Library of Congress Cataloging-in-Publication Data is available.

ISBN: 978-1-68556-072-0

E-ISBN: 978-1-68556-073-7

This is dedicated to my wife, Jackie, my kids, and the staff of New Life. You mean more to me than words can say.

Table of Contents

Foreword

In 2008, Hurricane Katrina sent ocean water rushing over the levees, destroying major parts of New Orleans, displacing millions of residents, and killing more than 1,800 people. The Galveston Hurricane of 1900 took even more lives. When the storm came inland, 8,000 people who chose to ignore the warning swept out to sea. Had they understood what was coming, they would have chosen differently. Likewise, on December 26, 2004, sailors either didn't see or didn't pay attention to the small bulges on the water's surface. The one-foot swells were barely noticeable in the enormous Indian Ocean. But as waves reached the shallow coastlines, the sea began to rise dramatically, eventually unleashing fifty-foot waves and killing about 200,000 people.

The energy released by the Indian Ocean tsunami was estimated to be the equivalent of 23,000 Hiroshima-type atomic bombs. What started out as a one-foot wave grew to become one of the deadliest natural disasters in history. Storms are inevitable! I've experienced my fair share of storms both in ministry and life. From the three miscarriag-

es my wife and I suffered to a brain hemorrhage that near-
ly cost me my life, the betrayal of friends, and then most
recently, the death of a younger brother who overdosed. I
remember hearing early on, in my walk with Jesus, church
leaders saying, "If you are in right standing with Jesus, you
will never have problems!"

This is simply not true. Scripture is full of examples of
godly people who experienced trials, storms, and suffering through no fault of their own. If your life seems over-
whelming to you right now and you don't know what to do
or how to handle it, you are not alone. There are thousands
of other people who feel trapped in their circumstances and
think they can't escape. But, the one thing I have learned
over and over is that God is good in the valleys and the
mountain tops. In life, we often find ourselves not knowing
what to do when faced with trials and storms.

This book is the perfect guide for those uncertain situations. "God of Both" explains how to have the kind of faith
that perseveres in trials, resists temptation, responds obedi-
ently to God's Word that produces good works. Don't get
me wrong—I still wrestle with being overwhelmed by the
challenges of life. But I now have a much better perspective
about how to deal with the circumstances when they come

my way. My prayer is that after reading this book, you will as well.

Landon won't be able to offer you three easy steps out of your difficult situation, nor will he share a magical prayer that will suddenly make everything better. However, I do believe—and it is my prayer–that each chapter of this book will bring you closer to victory—to a place where you are hopeful, not hopeless; peaceful, not stressed; and free, not overwhelmed. Jesus has chosen to work through people like Landon. Christ appears in his face, resolve, attitude and joy. He makes the rest of us want to love Jesus in the manner he loves Jesus. I pray you will read this entire book. And when you do, I'm convinced you will trust, love, and follow Jesus in both the mountaintops and the valleys.

—Steve Abraham
Senior Pastor, New Life

Introduction

It's His story; I'm just living it.

My life so far has been filled with good and bad. Peace and trauma. Rocky roads and rich moments. Crazy seasons and tranquil moments. Sound familiar? We all have parts of our lives we regret and some we wish we could forget altogether. But to wish that implies we don't want the bad parts, just the good. Honestly, it would be a great life to have no bad days. The truth is, in that view, we are accepting some of God's plan and rejecting some of His plan.

The responsibility that lies on our shoulders is that we must accept all of His plan, not just the good parts. I'm not saying God was the reason you got struck with that horrible diagnosis or that God caused the car accident that took their life. I'm just saying God uses *both*. The celebration and the grief. The regret and the lesson learned. God doesn't look at us and ask, "Do you want the good or the bad?"

I wish I could promise you a life full of only the good, but that just doesn't happen. What God does offer is, "I'll use *both* your good and bad days." It's not "or" anymore (never has been); it's both. This shift in your mindset can change everything, where nothing is wasted. Where regret no longer has its power over you because you know that God will use your worst mistakes and best decisions. He will use both.

We see time and time again of characters in our Bible who actually lived and walked and talked with Him thousands of years ago who made decisions that He redeemed. He redeemed a prostitute and included her in the family line of Jesus. He redeemed an adulterous king who should have been away at war with all the other kings. The same God we read about is still alive and redeeming horrible decisions today. He's done it over and over.

Am I saying we should go about our lives and make a fool out of ourselves? Far from that, what I am proclaiming from these pages is that you can look at your past failures, present anxieties, and future plans through the scope of both, trusting that God is going to use all of it, that nothing is wasted and nothing is forgotten. Picture a toolbox filled with every tool you needed; now imagine it half-full. That's living life through the lenses of just the good days. Bad days ultimately teach you ways that you really would not have learned while life was sunshine and rainbows.

Paul, the figure in the New Testament who wrote most

of what we read now, told you and me that everything in our lives, good and bad, would be used by God for His glory. God uses all of it. Every season and every second. Pain and purpose. The corruption and the calling. The limping and leading. The mess and the miracle. The negative and the positive. You have to understand that there are two sides to everything-heads and tails, what was said and what actually happened, the win and the loss.

As much as this narrative is about God being God in your bad days, glorious moments, and everything in between, it's more about God being God while you're in pain and when those dark seasons persist when you wish they would pass while you're lost, while you're invisible. Bad days come and go, but those internal states truly don't seem to give us a break. That's what this book is all about. To know and to be confident that God is working through you and in you, and in that season of drought, He's turning it around for your good and His glory.

Life, as we traverse through it, is filled with different sides of just about everything. Fortunately for us, God is on both sides of everything too. He's evident, and His glory is still prevalent in and through your life and my own. He is never truly done with us and our lives, and He is near in those moments and days of hurt, heartache, and pain.

We often try to speak in an "or" dialogue when in reality it is almost always "and." God doesn't waste a single moment, and neither should we. Through my short journey so far on this side of eternity, I now know that God is working for my good and using all the bad. He doesn't dispose of the bad—yes, He dealt with our sin issue on the cross—but we still have issues here today. Those parts come out in traffic.

Throughout these pages, you will see what this is all about, and I carry the conviction that the words you will read, if applied, will change your life. He is the God of both the mountaintops and valleys. Valley-living typically has a way of choking all the hope out of your life, beating you down until your crawling with no strength left in your bones. There are some things, though, that you really cannot learn without the valley.

On the other hand, we have those invigorating mountaintop experiences. Life is good, and God is good. Your career is matching your calling, the SUV is paid for, the debt is paid off, and you're living well. Mountaintop living has the tendency if we aren't careful to forget all that God is and what He is doing. More often than not, we are taking everything for granted, and what is taken for granted is usually stripped from us.

I have had both, and more often than not, I feel like I am valley-living and seeing those around me trek their way up to the mountaintop. While the struggle to balance work, marriage, kids, and everything else is beating me down, I have to remind myself that God is the God of both. He is going to use your good and bad days. Horrible seasons and plentiful harvests. Fragmented internal states and collected strengths. This is freedom. This is a way to really look at the sovereignty of the Architect of this life, that He is it all taken care of.

Our bad days exist to shape us and mold us, and without them, we would not be who God has called us to be. Can I encourage you to do something? It doesn't make a lot of sense, and it might be challenging and downright painful, it was for me. Begin today to thank God for the bad days, moments, and seasons in your life and watch your perspective come alive.

Now the question remains for us, if you're asking it, is this; is the book I'm holding in my hands for me? Whether you're fifty-four and nearing a midlife crisis because you thought you'd be farther along by now, this is for you. God will still use the days ahead of you, and your former days will not be greater than your latter days. If you're twenty-one and just finishing school, worried about what the future holds, these pages are for you too. God can use this story to help your perspective as your dark seasons come and you don't know where to turn. Quite frankly, it's not a coincidence you're about to embark on these next chapters; they'll help you along the journey as they have helped me.

The personal stories you will read on these pages are an invitation into my complicated and messy mind and life. To be quite honest, some of them were almost cut from this book, but I was reminded that there is power in the personal, no matter how embarrassing or shameful they might be. This is the path God has given me. My hope for you in our time together is that you will have a renewed hope and an invigorated new outlook on life. What my prayer for you is that this is a new journey for you, that you will begin again to love God and love people, and know that God will use both to better you and to mold you into who you're becoming.

1

Pain and Purpose

The path to our purpose is through our pain.

Do you remember those sayings people would speak over you as a kid? "She is just like her mother. He is built like a linebacker." What was yours? We all have had words spoken over us. We just have to pick which ones are actually truth and what are actually smoke. In full disclosure, mine was, "He really wears his heart on his shoulder." It took me a decade to truly understand what that meant. Looking back in full review, I can see those tendencies that bred that.

In life, it really does take you moments to look back and take precious inventory of the events and experiences that have transpired from your first day. All of our lives are filled with moments in space and time that have made you, you. Not one segment was skipped by God either, where we mess up is failing to invite God in on the process that He began in the first place. Obviously, it would be heresy to say God started the cancer in your body and that now has metastasized to your lungs and liver. That's not God; that's the fruit of the fallen world we live in. We just happen to blame God for it when in reality, we should turn our blaming into believing.

Believing in the God who watches us while we sleep and believing in the God who rescues people today, though we cannot see Him, requires faith. To see this Jesus that is spoken about in this narrative requires faith in the face of doubt. God knew we would struggle with doubt, and yet He meets us in the middle of the sea just like He met those He was closest to Him. In this story? He actually commanded them to cross the sea on His very word, and here they are, struggling to even get past the waves and the wind, yet He was about to reveal Himself as the God of the storm and the God of the stillness.

He's your personal God, in your storm, and in your stillness; He's the same. He uses both to reveal His character to you in light of the pain you're feeling or the purpose you're diving into. Allow me to explain. It takes the storms in your life to show Himself as the peacemaker. On the other side, it takes the disease in life to show Himself as Healer. He's both, and life will take you through both to show you the God I have had the amazing opportunity of following now for some time. All that to say, He is in your life—even now.

We may not know each other and our past experiences, and you most definitely will never have the probable chance of showing me the resume to your pain (we can try sometime, though), but we can share the same belief in the God who makes mountains hills and valleys vibrant with life. I know this because He did it with mine, and He will do it with yours. Now, back to the tendencies that make me, me.

Growing up, we watched tons of movies. Quite frankly, sometimes, I'm not sure how we got away with some of them. As a young kid, I didn't have a ton of community around me, so my family really became my only friend. Fridays were really my favorite day, not because of the weekend but because my dad would come home with two or three movies to watch. Ecstatic would be an understatement, especially because for most of his life, we had the same taste: guns blazing, car chasing, bad guy losing type of stuff.

One or two in particular that I can remember would slowly begin to pull those emotions you forget you even had or you didn't even realize were inside you. The person dies. The dog falls ill. In school, we all gathered around at the end of the year to watch one movie that we had been reading about, and honestly, if we were in a horror movie, I would have been found out by my slight suppressed sobbing in the back of my fourth-grade class. As I've aged, I have realized I just *feel*.

My feelings are directly related to my love for people, and here is the kicker—people cause pain. Are people the problem? Never will be. The moment we look at people as the problem, we lose ground in our unity and bond. People are loved and created by God, yet we have the tendency to cause pain. Directly or indirectly.

Have you ever felt that pain caused by a relationship? We aren't meant to live in a constant state of pain; that would be weird. Typically though, when we enter into any relationship, partnership, or fellowship with anybody, we are saying, "I want this and all the pain involved." When we accept people as they are, we accept the good and the bad, not the good or the bad.

Trying to just accept the good in people will end in disappointment for you, and trying to accept the bad in people will cause emotional instability either in you or the other party. This is typically known as manipulation, and the world needs less of that. Manipulation is the desire to control somebody in the belief that they will conform to your image of them. Thank God that we have a Savior who didn't try to manipulate us into His image, albeit we were already created in His image—we were just loved as we were.

You're loved just as you are, and you can go to the Master with your weird and jacked-up tendencies, knowing full well that He will love you through them. The guarantee? Don't expect to stay that way. God's love changes people; we know that because you might have experienced that or have yet to feel that but take it from the person giving you these words onto paper right now. I'm confident that He will do it with you as He did it with me. God has a high and eternal expertise in changing people who are far from Him.

He's done it with the adulterous husband in your complex; He's done it with the insecure woman down the row from you. He'll do it again, too. Often I have found that those who are farthest from God right now really are the ones that eventually are brought near to Him. We know this to be true because He did it with a man who was shorter in stature and found in the great narrative of God's love to us.

Crowds

We are introduced to this character in the Gospels, his name was Zacchaeus, and he was known as a chief tax collector. In other words, he was hated, and he was wealthy due to his profession. Yet, he knew deep down there was something, or Someone, calling him to a higher way of living. Through this story, we really do discover another layer of Jesus we haven't been introduced to yet. As it unfolds, this man who is hated by most for his profession is drawn near by the Man who claimed to be God. It took a high tree for him to climb so he could see over the crowd, yet Jesus knew this man. The Bible never records an initial interaction with these two, so we can assume this is their first moment together, and what does Jesus do? Calls him by his name in the midst of the crowd. That's Jesus.

I can still remember my first concert. It was in downtown Atlanta at a renovated tabernacle, and it's honestly where I began to fall in love with people who did not look like me. My best friend had introduced me to a certain genre of music that isn't for the faint of heart, and the people that listen to it are stereotypically covered in tattoos.

The smell of cigarettes was thick in the air, and the smell of sweat. In the middle of these melodies being played and choruses being strummed and sang to, people would gather in the middle of the room and throw hands, literally.

Men were the size of Goliath to me at the feeble age of sixteen. One misguided elbow would have guaranteed me a new set of teeth. Clueless by nature, I stumbled into the middle of this vicious room of death and smoke, and by God's great grace, I dodged a few elbows in time to get to the outer rim of this pit. Hundreds of people gathered in this one location to sing, to dance, to commemorate great music, and not one of them, besides my friend, knew my name. I didn't know theirs, either. But God does.

He knows your name too. Do you feel overlooked? Do you feel missed? Do you feel unheard? Do you feel lost in the crowd? He knows, and He sees, and the best news of all, He is coming to you. Straight to your situation and position, and He's got one thing to say: your name. This identified the man by all of his good qualities and all of his bad qualities, and we all have them. Yet, Jesus chose this man when he himself was rejected by the crowd around him. Jesus chose both.

My wife, Jackie, did not choose to marry me off my good conscience or my bad habits; she got both. It would be impossible to have married me off of my good behavioral traits and leave the bad eggs out of it. She accepted it and chose me anyways. God knew exactly what you would be drawn to, the good and the bad, and still chose you and loved you. He knew you long before your first mistake, and He plans on never leaving you through your most deliberate ill-willed decision. He's the God of both.

As life goes on, there is really only one real reason that shows me why God put me here in this moment in time— to love people. Yes, to love Him and love people. If you choose to directly love Him but not His creation, you're not following His direction. The more that we fall in love with people, we will discover our purpose and plan. As well as discover pain.

The two go hand-in-hand. Pain and people. Purpose and pain. It's both. Those closest to me have caused me the most pain, yet I still love them as they are. Take heart today that God loves you as you are, not as you should be. He can't wait to see you living in the way that He had in mind, but until then, He is ever patient and loves you exactly as you are. Do we intentionally let them take advantage of us?

No, that is downright unhealthy. We just continue to do the best we can with what Jesus taught you and me, to love and forgive without limits. Please don't let the abuse continue any longer, please tell somebody what you're dealing with or who wronged you or even who you wronged, but we must never stop forgiving.

You and the person that is causing you this pain right now are worth unlimited forgiveness. It doesn't run out; an endless well. In other words, God has been grieved a lot. More times than we can count, and His obsession is still people. He has never given up on loving you. It will always be people. We are the only beings He created in His likeness. We are His sole devotion.

So, what is our purpose here? To love people. Through the pain and disappointment they caused. It really is baffling when you look at it like this because we are called to love those who cause us the greatest amount of pain. The pets can cause pain, your job can cause pain, but no pain compares to that of those who you love with your whole heart. This is why it's so crucial to love well and forgive well. We aren't supposed to light a fire to every relationship in our lives that causes us pain and turmoil but to build from it, love from it, and keep on staying.

Sunday afternoons were the worst in our family. How about yours? As far as I can recall, there was certainly always a fight in our car on the drive home from church. My brother, Jamie, had a way of crawling under the skin of my parents, and they would lash out. My dad had a very loud, robust voice and in that scenario, surround sound had nothing on this cinema. Usually, the quarrel would begin with *Dad v. Brother*; then, my mom would be pulled into it. *Dad and Mom v. Brother.*

Sometimes though, as we peeled back on the onion of the fight, we realized my brother really wasn't the primary suspect. I can't blame my parents, though; they were doing the best they knew how. As the wedding bands would fly (it happened once, the finger was stripped of the ring and threw it at the windshield), words would clash, and by the time we got back to the house, it looked as if we just got out of a warzone.

The world is like that today. We are all in a tightly packed vehicle together, just yelling at each other because we have too much pain flying around. Here's the truth, we can't hear everybody because we think they are the obstacle in front of our purpose, and they are causing us our pain. Yet, as we look at it again, it's just a jumbled pile of words, and we have forgotten how to speak to one another. We are all experiencing the backseat of a car with a tumultuous amount of tension, and we are all riding together in the same direction.

But this is purpose and pain. God put me in my family for a reason. Same for you. God is so specific. He placed you in your family for something. The kicker? Your placement in your family is bigger than you. We miss the objective when we reject this, and in reality, we are telling our amazing, infinite, all-loving God that He was wrong. Sounds absurd, doesn't it?

We do it all the time. Yet, God doesn't make mistakes. If God made mistakes, He wouldn't be God anymore. This could be the time that you look in the mirror of yourself, your family, and your faith and accept both: the shipwrecked family and the purpose behind it.

Jackie loves baking but what it does is make a mess of the kitchen in our apartment. After the sugar, the dough, the batter, the utensils, and the wrappings, she usually has made something delicious. This is what it takes, though, a kitchen that is messed up and dirty to make something worth tasting. Your family might look like that, but that is what makes you unique. After all the trauma, the abuse, the lies, and the pain, you're still here, and your family is here, and on the other side of it, it'll be something worth sharing around a table.

Silence

Back to the Sunday McGarry circus, I really don't know if it's a middle child bend or the fact that we moved around a ton (I attended at least six or seven different elementary schools from what I can remember), but I was always observing and never speaking. One thing I do know is this: silence is almost always the wisest avenue to pursue. As my family erupted in chaos on those drive homes, I would stare out the window of the car.

I was never speaking or saying anything. Just staying silent as the flames got hotter and the storm grew darker. Until one day, my parents looked at me from the passenger seat and said, "Landon, say something!"

To this day, raising my voice in the volume that occurred that afternoon hasn't happened since. In a way, they gave me permission to speak up. We have the permission to speak up to injustice and stay silent when the situation calls for it. To shout and stay silent, we need both, and we need the discernment to dictate which one we will need to use.

Do you need permission to speak up? If you can do it in love, then you have full discretion to speak.

Looking at the life of Jesus, He shows us that in most circumstances, silence is the valuable, necessary option. When we choose silence, we immediately reject the possibility of anger, rage, or hatred spewing from our mouths. Silence is a muscle, honestly. The more you and I learn to use it, the stronger it can become. Jesus was silent in the very face of His enemies, and we can model that same lifestyle.

On the other hand, we need to speak up. But we do not speak up in violence or hatred. We speak up in love. If you plan on speaking up, but it is not based on love, it's not going to work. In other words, words spoken in hate have never motivated anybody to change. There is never a time for a harsh word. Rather, in the moment of love being spoken by a loved one or valued friend, we change. We understand. Only love has that power to motivate us to change.

So now the question is this, do I speak up, or do I stay silent? Practically you can use this tool to help guide you. Ask yourself, "Do I possess the ability to speak up in this situation or conversation in love? Is what I am going to say be a response instead of a reaction?" If you can wholeheartedly answer yes, then speak like your life depends on it. If you cannot, stay quiet and don't react.

As a father to two daughters, I am learning more and more how to speak up in love as a response, not a reaction. Reactions damage, responses build. Reactions typically breed remorse or regret, but responses tell another story. When Charlotte, our oldest, pours a bottle of water on a paper plate for no reason at all, I must respond and not react. Thank God for His grace because sometimes I want to lose my mind. We are works in progress, after all.

Can we begin to respond instead of reacting? Can we begin to build instead of destroying? My dad was great at many things; reacting was one of them and almost always resulted in a situation that was elevated in tension than one that relieved the issue at hand. Nobody else can do it for you; you have to make the decision to respond. Respond in the face of hatred, criticism, and negativity.

One of my most favorite quotes to date is about purpose, and one of my most favorite albums is about purpose. Purpose is filled with pain; yours, mine, and the other guy down the street from you. We cannot outrun it, and we really cannot ignore it. Pain, though, is a tool. A necessary one if we are going to love and live to our fullest extent. You see, pain, when applied to pressure and our purpose, creates passion.

Passion really is what separates the ordinary from the extraordinary. The path to passion is only through pain. We all notice the difference between a normal barista and a passionate one, a passionate salesman and a regular one. It separates the good from the really good. The saddest thing to me, though, is when somebody who claims to follow Jesus just does not carry passion, where they spend their life, in season after season, called monotony.

Monotony is the breeding ground for more monotonous episodes. From how we feel pain, we have two choices. To know that this pain is pointing me to my purpose or a dead end. Have you ever been tired of the way life is going? Same job, same car, same house, year after year? Please hear me; I am not saying pack your bags and move across the country or divorce your spouse. That is never the option. It all comes down to your perspective, and your perspective is precious—a perspective that can stare in the face of the ordinary.

God is in the small things as much as He is in the big

things. We get so used to dreaming and seeing Him in the big that we really forget that the King of kings goes with us to the gas station too. We need to adjust our perspective daily because if we do not, we will fall into that endless cycle of routine, and the routine kills passion, and when your passion has died, you become an empty shell.

What's the reason we get in so much trouble? We get bored. It could be said that King David got into a lot of trouble because he got bored. How do you fight boredom? Go after people and discover your unique purpose through pain. Pain will shock you back into life. Have you ever been cooking, and all of a sudden, your hand touches that searing hot pan? It brings you back to life. Pain does that, and it's a blessing.

Did you just read pain and blessing in the same sentence? God is the God of both. When Jesus was hanging on the cross in pain that we cannot even begin to imagine, He became the greatest blessing to all of us here on earth that would ever live in the past, present, and future. He brought you and me back to the Father from what used to separate us from Him, sin.

What now? Through His death and resurrection, we can live this life in full view of our purpose and choose to love those closest to us who cause the most pain. We can choose today to choose silence; we can choose to love our neighbor and discover that our purpose will be discovered in this path called pain. You're going to face pain today or tomorrow; I can guarantee that much.

2

Broken and Blessed

What if the blessing is disguised in something broken?

Have you ever felt broken before? Heart wide open on the floor, even? Betrayed? Burned? Back stabbed? I'll never forget receiving a text that broke me wide open for the world to see. But first, here is the context for you. As I neared finishing high school, our family was a mess. We had just about everything going wrong that could go wrong and then some.

My dad, who we can say was the primary staple of the family, had left for a business trip, and that left me at home with my mom, who had a raging problem with adult beverages. Some people are happy when the bottle is in place, and then others are, well, my mom. She was always on vengeance when she let that bottle hit her lips, and I was stuck in our small camper where we were living at the time. When my dad left, it was my mom's moment to have a few. After a few nights, I couldn't bear it much longer because I

needed my sleep, and my mom was drinking well throughout the night.

This is for those who have seen and witnessed firsthand
the problem of addiction in your family and your close
loved ones. It's evil, and sometimes, it's really like there is
no hope until they themselves want it. Small reminder for
you and me: we cannot change people. We may be desperate for them to change, which in all honesty is healthy,
but we cannot initiate that change. They do. Sometimes it
might take rock bottom, and other times, it might require a
funeral until they change.

After a few days at the local restaurant where I waited
tables, I had a colleague drive me home, and I was at my
wit's end with the situation. Pulling into the gravel parking
space for our car, it was evident this would be a night like
the past few. Approaching the camper, I knew this was the
night I would have to leave for good. No surprise to anybody as the door swung open that booze was had and rage
was being served for dessert.

In a swift moment, I grabbed what I could and left.
Sometimes you need to leave where you were to go where
God is calling you. Like Abraham. In a way, I haven't
stopped thanking God for how it happened because, with-

out the discomfort and pain, I would probably still be in that small town. Pain has a way of pushing you out of the comfortable into the wide-open spaces that God has for you. Pain has a unique way of pulling what is inside of you, out of you.

Are you in a season of enhanced pain? Unbearable, even? It might be high time that God is on the move, and He is about to bring something beautiful out of it. It takes pain to birth a child. It takes pain to get your muscles to grow. It takes pain to get to the healing. Pain is, unfortunately, a necessary tool that we all must have so that in God's hands, it'll be used for His glory. Back to the story.

Unfortunately, due to the circumstances we were in, I did what I had to do, couch surf. If you have ever couch surfed before, you know what this is pointing to. You're always at the mercy of the opposing party and almost guaranteed discomfort on the daily. My time to go to Bible college was approaching slowly, and because of that, I was trying to save every bit of money that I could. This meant cutting corners.

We aren't called to cut corners as Christians. Every time you cut that corner, take the short route when you know you were supposed to take the long one; you circumnavigate God's plan for you and your character. Will God use it? Of course. But we need not take the detour when the road itself isn't even broken. My friend was so gracious to set me up in the basement of his place, and the time came for rent, a price I couldn't and wouldn't pay.

Doing what I knew best (three and a half couches earlier), I packed my bags and left again. Shortly thereafter, I received a text that changed my whole day and season for a short while later. To put it plainly, it basically excommunicated me from the family forever, all the while going after my character.

Remember, cutting corners will cost you. It will cost you relationships and bridges that never needed to be burned in the first place. I was broken. Have you ever felt broken before? God works in broken places and brings blessings that we cannot even begin to imagine or think of. God is God; He really can make beauty from ashes. There's a story in my Bible of a kid with a lunchbox who had to feed thousands of people.

As the story goes, Jesus breaks the bread, and it blesses each and every person in the crowd. Before the bread could be a blessing, though, it *had* to be broken. This isn't to be public enemy number one right now, but you're going to need to be broken. Often I have found that those who resist the breaking are rejecting the blessing. It's both. When we are broken and fragmented, it paves the way for the light to come in and heal us.

God is really good at using broken people for His mission in the world. Your broken places do not disqualify you from His love either. We have too many people in the church today who claim to love Jesus but dislike and are utterly disgusted with broken people forgetting that at one point in time, God picked them up from their own mess and brought them back together. Here is the key though, for all of us, we aren't meant to stay broken. Our responsibility is to find healing no matter what it takes so that we can be the hands of Jesus in the lives of broken individuals in our lives and be part of the mending in their lives too.

Jesus was broken for you. Yes, you. The broken, addicted, angry and nasty version of you. Before Jesus could do what He came to do on this planet, He had to be broken before He was the ultimate blessing. What was that? Forgive humanity for its err and wrong. You need to discover that forgiveness and grace. It'll change your life.

The fastest way to stay broken and the way to stay that way is to never forgive yourself. God hasn't called you to hate yourself; He never has. Yeah, sure, hate what is wrong with you and always go after the person He created you to be, but never hate yourself. One preacher said it this way, "When you doubt the product, you insult the manufacturer." My Maker made me; why would I hate that? We do it all the time.

We endlessly replay those episodes in our own lives of moments we aren't proud of. We hit rewind all the time, but God is beckoning you to live this life victoriously, and those memories are destroying you. We all have baggage we aren't proud of. The truth of the matter is that we have all grieved God more times than we can count and He is always right there, welcoming us with open arms of forgiveness and grace for you and your mistake.

We hate ourselves because we can't accept the wrong things. It's that horrible decision you made in high school, and you keep replaying it in your head. When you accept them, you acknowledge the problem, and once the problem has been identified, healing can begin. This is crucial for you to do. Once you find your healing in the Person of Jesus, you can become a blessing. It's your choice now, choose that free gift of acceptance and forgiveness and see the blessing and be the blessing, or don't.

What are we really discussing? Regret. Regret is poison for us, and we drink it daily. You never become who God has called you to be while living in a constant state of regret. So often, what happens is we put regret on this pedestal and give it more power than that which the cross did for us, which eliminated the debt that we had. The death of Jesus defeats the power of regret over your life and mine. It's time to live in freedom; God is calling you to something higher.

Pieces

Here is what is true in this life, you and I are a complicated collection of pieces. We have pieces of us from our childhood called trauma and abuse, and we have pieces from us right now called insecurity and pain. We consist of pieces, which make us who we are. Typically only you can see your pieces, and sometimes your pieces are evident to everybody around you.

Your pieces are what make you who you are. Unfortunately, our pieces aren't the most fitting for our own psychology and personalities, but God knew them all along.

Long before you would breathe your first breath, He knew your pieces, and that's what makes you beautiful. Did you know that? What makes you who you are is your entire life's experience thus far.

In all of your fragments and shards, you're a masterpiece. God doesn't make messes; He makes masterpieces. We make a mess of ourselves with our own dumb decisions, but God in His sovereignty is making something beautiful out of you and your life. You were put in your family for a reason. This generation was supposed to have you in it. We can't see the beauty in our pieces at the moment, but by living our lives in reverse, we can see that God's hand was working on our behalf.

Growing up in a small town in Georgia and looking back over my life, I can see the pieces He was putting together for the life I am living right now. We have to look back over our lives, collect the pieces and present them to God and watch how He works. We don't have to understand all of the darkness, but we can be sure that God is going to do something with our pieces.

Now the question poised for us here is, what do I do with the pieces in the meantime? Namely, in the process of our past and present, what do we do with the fragments?

For one, we don't stab each other. The pieces that you possess are not meant for the detriment of your neighbor. We are not called to pick up our shards and use them as weapons against the poor cashier at the coffee shop.

Your shards do not give you entitlement to be a jerk to anybody in your path. At all costs, we must rid ourselves of this weapon called entitlement. On this journey called life, I have discovered that God doesn't owe you anything. He doesn't owe you an explanation for your past pain; He doesn't need to explain Himself for the horrible car accident that took that beloved family member.

He didn't author that car accident; He didn't write that cancer into your body; this broken world did. We live in a fallen world, and in this shattered life, things just happen. When we accept that things just happen, we can wield the hope that good things can take place too. Throughout it all, though, God doesn't owe you anything, and when you come to that conclusion for yourself, entitlement has no place.

If God didn't do a single thing the rest of history, the cross was enough for us. The cross was and is enough for your pain, your trauma, your attitude, and your regrets. The next time you are staring at that poor cashier at the coffee shop, remember that entitlement will only make the situation worse for you and them. It wasn't the barista's fault that you had a bad morning, and it wasn't your fault that you experienced that pain from your family member growing up.

What matters now is, can we take ownership over all our pieces? You can. It's called owning your story or, in another "churchy" word, your testimony. You have one, and I have one that is specific only to you. Make it personal. When you make it personal, your story becomes powerful. The world needs more people who are willing to stand up and take ownership of their stories. Own it, your story, and all that makes you, you. This is the word of extreme caution for us here today though, either you own your story, or your story will own you.

This is called becoming the victim. You are not a victim. There will be more on this in the coming chapters, but it's worth stating now. You are not your past. You are not what you did to yourself or what others did to you; you are a victor. There was a season, a long one, where I played the victim. "It's their fault I am walking through this; it's my parents' fault that I wasn't set up for success." That cassette called victim was on replay, and all it did was keep me stuck in the same loop with no advance forward.

It's time you reject that cassette, that loop of bad thinking, and take extreme ownership over your life. Yeah, that mistake or decision happened, but we move on from it and learn from it and get better from it, not worse. God did not create a bunch of victims; He created conquerors. He created participants. Jesus, in His final hours, could have played victim to Judas, but He chose to own it.

You see, for the joy that was set before Him, He knew exactly what He was about to walk through and walked through it as a victor and not a victim. He didn't curse Judas on that cross; He forgave Judas on that cross—He forgave you too. Not one day was left outside of His sight, and with His redeeming grace, you can get up from reading this book and know that you can live a life of victory. But it takes forgiveness.

Forgiveness takes courage, and it might be the hardest thing you have ever done. Forgiving is something God does, and it's also something, through Jesus, we are taught how to do. Jesus forgave you, and we are meant to go forgive those who have hurt us. Does this mean allowing the behavior? Definitely not. It means you forgive them so you can release them and live the life ahead of you.

Grudges

Allow me to illustrate this for you with the complicated and messy life who is penning this to you now. Shortly after my senior year of high school, life was hell. We had some traumatic experiences all the while the parents of yours truly were in the beginning experience of their divorce. This had been whispered about through conversations as I aged, but now the gavel had been slammed, and both parties were ready to split.

Years later, the lack of forgiveness I see is horrendous. Phone calls are filled with "he said, she said," and there doesn't seem like common ground will ever be found. This might be a mouthful, but some peace between loved ones will never be found until we meet in eternity all together. This encourages me because I know we live in a frail and faulty world. You are not responsible for every relationship in your life where there is no forgiveness. You're solely responsible for you and the forgiveness that you offer to those who have hurt you or even that you hurt them.

In the present day, the evil that has so saturated itself is sad. It's a daily struggle for me to watch and hear, and in most moments, I do have to turn off the phone and refuse to respond to the text message. Not every reaction deserves a response. There's more on that in a later chapter. A holy word of caution, whatever you refuse to let go of will fester and grow and develop, and eventually, it's going to harm you more than the initial incident.

Can you imagine the weight that would fall from every life in this world if they dropped the baggage of what happened to them? The truth is we are all weighed down by something or what someone did to us. God has been impressing on your heart for some time now to drop the weight and leave it, never to pick it up again. You can experience forgiveness and freedom. You can be set free for the rest of your life from that grudge that has been held inside of you all this time.

Shortly after my wife and I celebrated two years of marriage, we had a morning that I will never forget. No, not amazing sex. We had just had Charlotte, our firstborn, and I had a dream. Please know, I am not one of "those" people who analyze every dream, but this one was a little different. To each his own, for me, God just speaks differently. If you have been married long enough, too, you know that your spouse does a really good job (not always) of speaking for

God.

As I woke up, I explained to her this dream I had just had of my dad.

"You should call him," Jackie spoke. In my own prideful thoughts, there was no way I was about to call him. Not necessarily out of anger or hatred; I just didn't have the desire. Only half an hour passed before I was ringing him. My dad is a character and as strong as a horse, and he loves to talk. Time passed, and I knew what needed to be said.

"Hey, Dad, I just want to thank you for the life you provided us kids growing up." Slowly the lump in my throat got bigger, and tears flowed down my face. This was the first time I intentionally thanked him for all he did for his family; this was the first time I took ownership over my life. Did my dad cause a lot of the pain we experienced? Yes. Ultimately was he trying his best? Of course. You have to understand that he was fathered by his dad, whose dad walked out on him with zero relationship.

Dad was just doing the best with what he had. How differently we would all be if we decided to look at both sides like God does. God doesn't just look at your horrible side or your narcissistic side like we, finite beings, do to one another; He looks at both and uses both. It might be time for you, friend, to look at both sides of your story and begin to acknowledge that you may or may not be proud of who you are or aren't yet, but it's a start. God is all about progress, and He's in the process, and He is ever so patient and kind with us to help us figure out our stuff while He already has us figured out.

Since then, to be completely candid, it's been different. For so long, I was used to playing the victim card, but now I'm on the other side, on the victor side. We have to be careful, though, because we are not the hero in our story. We are just playing our part until we get to the finish line.

In all honesty, this might be the hardest thing you will ever do, but you need to pick up that phone, die to yourself and your pride, and begin to thank those who need no thanking. Please hear me, though; I am not talking about forgiving and forgetting, especially to those deep atrocities that there doesn't seem to be any place for forgiveness. We don't let people take advantage of us, but we can take advantage of forgiving and loving and thanking them in spite of all the pain and grief and heartache.

The blessing will be disguised in that phone call or text, or conversation. We can be blessed and broken all at the same time, but you can heal. You can be restored. God in

His nature is a Redeemer. He can redeem you, and He can redeem them. You can choose to thank God at this moment or curse God, but you'll be left better and stronger if you begin to state your thanks to God for all that He has done in your life and all that He is going to do. Now, pick up the phone.

3

Crawling and Cheering

We all can speak, but what're you saying?

Have you ever had a horrible day? One for the record books? In all honesty, I despise those silly quotes that are meant to inspire you, such as, "You have to have the bad days to enjoy the good ones." Shut up. Bad days are all around us and what is also around us keeps us crawling for life, harsh words. Through studying life from my own perspective, I have found out that there really is no place for a harsh word. A harsh word harms and hurts no matter who you are. Have you ever met anybody who felt helped after a harsh word?

What actually matters? Encouragement does. I hope you understand that to the very core of your being. Through social media and other outlets, we have stopped encouraging and have really begun to compare violently. Comparison will never do for you what encouragement can build. Comparison will steal your lunch money and laugh at you while you starve. We are meant to build people up and ourselves up. When people walk away from an interaction with you, are they left tired or full?

We have the power to change an entire day through one word. Bad or good. Life itself has a way of beating us down until we are crawling. The good news is we are all crawling; we have just learned to conceal it. We can encourage our neighbor while trying to find our footing; go ahead and try. Unfortunately, we are more isolated than ever before, and we have realized that isolation doesn't do anybody good mentally.

We have the keys through our own tongue to unlock blessing in somebody's day; it just takes practice and intentionality. You don't just "accidentally" encourage somebody; you seek them out at the grocery store or bank. The truth is, there is somebody in your day today that needs your encouragement because they have been crawling for quite some time. Life has a way of getting us down and keeping us down, and when we are down, we lose our focus on everybody else and put it on ourselves.

Proceed with caution; with the focus always and entirely on yourself, you will not be able to encourage those who are desperately needing your encouragement, love, and acceptance. This is why we, as Jesus' followers, believe this life is not about us; it's about Him. When we actively decide that, we become a source of encouragement for people because Jesus is an encourager.

How do you become an encourager? Looking around at everybody else and going to them. In my Bible, there's a story of a woman who we will name Sally, and Sally was a woman of the night. If you know what I am talking about, you know what I am talking about. She's been caught in the very act of adultery and is now in the midst of those who want her to pay for the crime she just committed.

The religious group of the day brought her to Jesus to see what Jesus would do. Almost as if He is ignoring their accusations, Jesus stoops down in the dirt and finally addresses them the way only Jesus can. His reply? Whoever is without guilt can cast the first stone. Jesus is our example to live by every single day of your journey here on earth. Follow closely.

He goes to Sally after all her accusers are gone and doesn't reprimand her; He loves her and encourages her. He doesn't give her a license to go back to adultery, He gives her a better way, and it is His way. So in this story, who are you? The accused or the accuser? Jesus has called us to live and be like Him as He is so are we.

Jesus didn't point fingers, and neither do we. We are never more like our enemy when we point our fingers. Pointing fingers create division and animosity, and rage. We are not the accuser in this story; we are the accused. We are so guilty of all the wrong we have ever done or will do, but Jesus comes onto the scene and changes everything.

This is the moment that all the changed people need to stand up and acknowledge they were once lost, but now they are found. We all were shoved to our knees by people or circumstances around us, and we were demanding justice for the accusations that were in fact justified, yet Jesus responded in a way we have never seen. According to the Mosaic law, this woman was destined for death but thank God the Divine interrupted this impromptu legal procession. He interrupted yours, too.

It's time we refuse to pick up the stone or, in modern-day terms, point the finger and go to the hurting and those struggling and begin to encourage them out of their sin and wrong ways. We do not endorse their sin; we encourage them out of it. How? Through identity. Identity is bred through words more than actions.

My daughters will have an identity formed and fashioned that is solely responsible from my mouth and Jackie's. We are in charge of forming their identity as they get older. You can speak straight to the identity of those crawling around you. They are counting on you to speak up in love and encouragement. The question remains for us here, if you do not speak it, who will?

People all around are crawling for dear life. Suicide is at an all-time high, prescriptions and medications are running wild, our screen time has increased by amounts unimaginable. You do not need to wait to stand to encourage those who are crawling right next to you. What a powerful image of two close friends just crawling through this life, all the while cheering for one another? We should treat our kind words like water, they are essential, and we are dying without them.

In my early twenties, I spent two years in Seattle. If you don't know, it rains. The first job I landed there was at a bank, and I would use the Kings County Public Transit System to get here and there, and that meant work. There is also something else that occurs in Seattle, and to be candid, it was worse than the rain. Seasonal moodiness hit me like a brick. Growing up, I actually enjoyed the gloominess of rain clouds without the rain, but in Seattle, I got both.

One particular day, on my way back home, it was a rough day. Anxiety through the roof, future was so out of sight and foggy, and I was so lonely. Have you ever felt like that before? Your future looked bleak, your mind was racing, and anxiety was at record levels? Today was one of those days.

As the bus approached my stop, I gathered my items and proceeded to step over the threshold, and this man, who was larger than life, met me in the rain, and I think my RPF (resting panic face) caught his attention. This is key. I do not remember what he said, but I do remember how he made me feel. He made me feel seen and not alone. In the midst of the rainy night, he met me where I was. A complete stranger and the interaction was a mere fifteen seconds at most.

You have fifteen seconds all day to meet people on their rainy days and uplift them. In our current season as humans, the rain has gotten heavy and loud. The thunder is deafening. We are dealing with stuff we never thought we would deal with. This global pandemic we are in at the time of this writing has driven people to their wit's end. Obviously, we cannot turn to the media for our encouragement—rather the opposite. We are left more hurt, more anxious, and more depressed with the media we live with today.

The rain is getting loud, but you know what can get louder? Our words. Our extremely intentional encouragement to people all around us who are counting on our words. Mental illness is running rampant, and we have forgotten who we are. We are in an identity crisis that is surpassing this epidemic. People are yearning to know who they are, and if we do not tell them who they are—loved and forgiven—who else will tell them?

Please hear me, though; this goes beyond just speaking nice and encouraging things to your neighbor. This is about speaking to yourself. What do you speak to yourself? Are you consistently battering yourself with horrible words? Is it a daily experience where you bully yourself over and over? This is your moment, your permission slip, to speak love and acceptance over yourself. In most cases, we are often the only ones who will truly encourage ourselves before anybody else does.

In a rather climactic scene in our biblical story, the great King David knew what it was to encourage himself. David had just returned to where he was and had gotten the bad report that the enemy had taken their wives and kids, and he was stuck between two bad reports; the stolen families and his own men deliberately discussing stoning him. Talk about discouraging. Yet, at this moment, he doesn't have a pity party and wallow in his guilt; he looks up and encourages himself in who God is.

Let that be for us today the example we follow in our lives. Look up. When your own mind is screaming at you, look up. When nobody else is around to encourage you, speak life to yourself. It's never the wrong time to encourage yourself and build yourself up. Can I tell you that your words will build yourself up faster than anybody else's will? It's time to contribute to the confidence that God is building within you by speaking to yourself what He has already declared, and His Word is final.

Paul wrote an amazing portion of Scripture and one in specificity speaks right to us here today, wherever you are reading this from. We were made to cry with those who cry and laugh with those who laugh. In other words, sympathy and empathy should run through our veins for the people in our lives. We should be running for our lives from apathy. What is apathy at its core? Refusing to feel the pain of our friends.

If you're a boss or manager in your field, choose sympathy and empathy. Lead with it. Hear from it. Speak to it. The colder this world gets, we can be the warmth that humanity is in need of. Whether you are a teacher, banker, grocery clerk, ministry leader, or politician, if you can decide to be more empathetic and sympathetic, we can begin to turn the heat up on this chilly planet.

We really should be known for our love and grace and acceptance. It should be what defines you in the morning and when you leave the office. Your money does not define you and cannot change the world; your 401k cannot help anybody; in reality, the pension from your retirement will not help change anybody; it's our love. It's always been about our love. Our love should speak from streets and the hallways. It should shout from the gas station attendant to the boardroom.

Breaking

The question remains for us here, do you feel like you're crawling? Barely holding on? Just getting through the day is your goal? Has your mind been attacking you? Are you at the breaking point, and you feel like you cannot even begin to encourage anybody in your path, including you? Our minds are a messy place.

Somebody once said that our mind is where most of life's battles are won or lost. Do you feel like you're losing yourself? Barely keeping your head above water? It's okay. You'll make it through. There is more to life than the emotion you're dealing with right now. Our emotions cannot be trusted, and you cannot be managed by those unstable inclinations.

There was a time in my life where my mind was brutally having its way with me. There would be nights that I thought to myself, "If I wake up this night, this is it." Suicide seemed to be knocking at my door, and the key to my mind was slipping into its hands. To be clear, these emotions never made their way into my life when I was young; it was as I aged.

Something doesn't want you to live this life, and it is going to be the fight of your life. Thank God for Jesus and His example set for us here today. In the narrative, He is found in a garden, and He is dealing with the fight of His life. Whether or not to go to the cross to die a death that we deserved, not Him. As the story goes, Jesus' own capillaries burst in this heated moment of prayer to the Father, and He is bleeding drops of blood.

Jesus kept His focus on the mission at hand, saving humanity and restoring that which was broken—our relationship with God the Father. Could it be that you are dealing with the mess of your mind because you have lost your focus? It's time to get it back. Focus on what is ahead, the dreams and aspirations you have, the family in your future, the career, and the calling in front of you.

It's all hinging on your focus. Focus on the right things, things that are noble, pure, true, holy, and right. The thing about your focus is I cannot fix it for you; only you can. When your focus is fixed, nothing else can fix your focus for you. There is so much in front of you, friend. You cannot end it at the breaking point. You must press on; you have to. We have heard it put it this way, "It's a permanent fix to a temporary problem."

Hurting people are all around, waiting on your word for them. Throw on your shoes, dust your knees off and crawl another day and while you're crawling, cheer your neighbor on. We can be the cheerleaders that raise the morale for a generation. There is no perfect moment to begin this decision to cheer somebody on while you yourself are crawling; what a beautiful image of a community of people who are all crawling yet refusing to give up on themselves or those next to them.

Your words matter to everybody you meet. Not one person is excluded from that. This is the moment you have been waiting for permission. Give yourself full permission to press on and cheer everybody on that you meet. You, sir, are not a police officer or, ma'am, you are not just an accountant. You're a holy cheerleader, equipped and empowered by God to spread and speak hope in the darkest hour.

At that moment, the haunting question proposed here for us is, if you're not speaking, who is? Who will speak for the downcast and broken? We know that in most circumstances, the critic is the last and the first to speak, but it doesn't have to be that way. Critics are valuable in that they actually show us where we need to love the most. It's a valuable question to repeat though, who will speak? The critic or the comforter and the person hanging in that balance are you and your words.

Currently, in my own life, I've only been in attendance at three funerals from my most recent memory. Two of which I carried the honor of being the minister to. One observation that carries consistently through the three, and

I am confident you have seen and heard the same, the kind and robust words of the deceased. People come together to weep, mourn, grieve, and celebrate the great divide we all must cross one day. Yet, we wait until the last day when that person we loved is no longer here.

Why do we wait? Why do we wait to encourage somebody until it's too late? When they are dead and gone? This might be heavy, but it's for us to consider; there are people dying all around us, and do you know what they are counting on? A word. There is precious power in your tongue, and we have two choices with those who are closest to us. The first option is we withhold the good word or the encouraging remark because we are fearful or downright prideful.

The second choice is we speak. We speak like life is literally coming out of our mouths. When I get to my casket or urn (whatever they decide to do with me), I want to get there spent. By that, I mean I don't want any kind words left in my vocabulary that was supposed to be shared. Our good intentions will never encourage people, but our actions and deeds and words will. Intent is great but let that intent breed action.

Many of us will get to eternity's door with intentions

and no action. Your intention cannot encourage somebody, but your deliberate action from that intention can. This is the whole scenario when you meant to send the text but didn't. The text never made it because our intent could not stir up the action. We must get past the intent and go directly into choices and actions that will encourage and inspire people.

There doesn't have to be another day that passes or dearly beloved that dies before we pick up our phone and call them and tell them how loved and valued they are. Do you know what this does? It changes the atmosphere. Have you ever noticed the difference somebody makes when they enter the room or when they leave the room?

Let us be the kind of people who light up every bus, conference room, hallway, and stairwell. In reality, the world around us is getting darker, but we can light up the human spirit by our tongues in action, refusing to quit. We'll either catch the attention of the world by our silence or by our speech, and we have to be the ones that make the decision.

4

Suffering and Serving

While we suffer, we can serve.

Around the world today, we are seeing and experiencing profound and emphasized pain and suffering on scales we haven't really witnessed before. Emotionally, it's hard to even process everything going on; floods in the southern states, typhoons over poorly developed nations, earthquakes rattling nations, and wildfires in my home state of California. Smoke is everywhere, and there are conversations being had that this is our new normal.

Really? The suffering of people groups and people of different nationalities is the new normal? That's a drastic change of affairs in our current predicament today. The blessing is in the statement, though. If we look at that statement in itself, "new," then that means it's been changed from the previous "normal." Whatever that "normal" is or was. This means it's interchangeable.

It's worthy of looking at this moment, though, and I

would like to propose that question to you, how're you suffering? We've briefly covered the world's chaotic eco- system, but this whole narrative is about you. It's about us. How're you doing? Really? We are all suffering in some measure today.

We can see that this is evident in the way we handle ourselves, speak to ourselves and approach the people in our lives. We are all suffering in the day and age we live, but here's the beauty in it; it means we are in this together. You're not alone in your hurt and heartaches. You're not fighting this fight on your own. You're with me, and I'm with you in it.

Sadly, suffering isn't anything new. Humanity has been dealing with the repercussions of sin and sorrow since the beginning of time. Suffering has always been the norm. But as we learned, if it's the "new" normal and it's technically not even the "new" normal but our normal state of life, then can something be changed?

Can we change it? God can. He can do it through us, too. He's God in the hurricane, and He's God in the di- vorce. Through the suffering of the loss of the child or pregnancy, and the woman who is ninety-eight on her death bed from good, old age, He's in both circumstances. Yet,

God changes things.

He's changed the unclean to clean. He's transformed the chemo into celebration as the cancer is no longer evident in the body. God changes everything in our world today. He changes it through available people who are ready to serve Him, and this is where it's crucial; while you suffer, you can serve. The globe today consists of changed people who are in the market to help in changing people. Remember with me, though; we personally cannot change people and suffering people at that. But, suffering is the gate to a change of life that only Jesus has to offer. Have you ever seen somebody lost in the woods?

That would be pretty sad because it means you saw them but didn't help them. Maybe you were lost somewhere at some point. What brought you out? The aid and help of a friend or even a complete stranger. Here is the beauty, we're all a bunch of suffering strangers, and we can help people and serve people in their suffering and our own.

The most detrimental party we can hold in the moment of our suffering is one that consists of pity. Yet, we can serve all the more. To be honest, our suffering should not drive us to our end but should drive us to our neighbor who is dealing with a broken-down car and needs some help that only you can offer. You are able to serve. You don't need a resume; you don't need prerequisites to serve your loved one or your community; you don't need a title, either.

What is the prerequisite really then to serve? It's our suffering. Suffering brings the world together if you haven't noticed. The media is really good at spinning fear and anxiety, but one thing they do correctly is the promotion of the floods and the winds and the aftermath of people coming together to search and scour the debris in hopes of finding life. Humans were created to serve. We were made by God to love Him and to love others. Loving is serving.

How does the debris look in your life right now? The debris has a way of clouding our view so that we cannot see our neighbors' pain, so we become selfish and try to clean up our own lives on our own, but this is where the truth is in service; serving is never done alone. We can serve others while the hospital bills stack up. You can serve your colleague at work while your loved one at home is dying of cancer.

Suffering makes the world go round, while serving enhances the spin. Nowhere are we told to stop serving while we are suffering; Paul actually fights this notion in the

Scripture. To put it simply for you, we can celebrate with those who are celebrating, and we can grieve with those who are grieving. It's both. There really isn't an antidote to our suffering next to the comfort of our Savior and what He brings to us, but serving has a peculiar way of deleting some of the pain attached to suffering.

Is it still going to hurt? Of course. We do it anyway. We press on anyway. We don't put a pause on people while our pain is hindering us. We pursue God, and He shows how to passionately pursue people and assist people and aid people.

People

At the heart of serving, the core of its being is people. Take a look around you, and you'll notice this. People are served at restaurants, and people are served at the baseball game. The great act of service is done throughout each day, all over the world. Industries and corporations are built around the act of service, yet the industry of service dates all the way back to when eleven guys believed the words of Jesus, and they themselves chose to believe in them too.

If the world does this, how much more should we, as Jesus' followers know this? Earlier in the chapter, we learned that this suffering is now known as the new normal, but if that's the case, it means we can change it. We can mold it into something beautiful and something of notable mention. With God inside of us, we have the power to change the world, to change nations, to change states, and to change people. Obviously, we can't change people, but God does, and He does it through our acts of service.

We serve people because we love people. We gather around Jesus with people. People are God's greatest possession. We are His. You are His. No amount of suffering we can feel or see or experience will ever separate us from this love that died for us.

A beautiful name that the Bible gives us of Jesus is that of, get ready for it, the Suffering Servant (surprise). Jesus knew what it was to suffer and to hurt and to bleed, but He also knew He couldn't stop there. People were His mission. They still are. He still seeks and saves the lost. He still goes out into pastures called nations and neighborhoods and finds people in their suffering, and He brings them home.

We can, too. The colleagues you work with every day are suffering from something, and we cannot be solely focused on our own pain and trauma that we miss our neighbor dealing with internal or external matters. As Jesus did, we can go to people and get in the mud with them, and through the trenches of depression and guilt, we can walk them through it.

This is the only chance we have to shift the state we are into something beautiful. There are a million opportunities a day to serve your fellow man and woman. All it takes is a moment to look up from your Smartphone or tablet and take note of all the people around you. What is this called? It's called being seen and seeing people.

People are missed every day because we are caught up in our bad days, and we are too self-focused on our own pain that we miss the very people in front of us who are hurting too. We are where we are because somebody in our lives, a grandparent or aunt, saw you and made you feel seen, and they assisted you as they themselves suffered. To be seen is to be valued, and to be valued is to be served. Every human being is worthy of service. Every person is worthy of love.

The suffering of our Savior still drove Him to serve His fellow disciples and the village leper. Jesus was mocked and ridiculed, and watch this, Jesus had feelings like you and I do. Jesus heard these names, and He heard the curses, yet He stooped low in the dirt for me. He did it for you, too. The only model we are called to follow and replicate is that of our very own Suffering Servant.

Suffering shows significance. Suffering brings you close to all things that matter in this life, God and people. While we suffer, we can approach our own people that have been intentionally placed in our lives, and we can serve them until our knuckles turn white. You see, we are all here because of One man who served us to the end and continues to serve us today. This story is why we are all here, and the life He lived and still lives is what inspired most of what you are reading.

Rags

As Jesus approached His final days of mortality on this side of heaven, He ate with friends, His closest disciples that witnessed the miraculous and His authority. They gathered together in a room, and there they enjoyed life, food, and good drink. Conversations came to a dim, and the only sound was that of the Man they knew getting down on His knees with a rag to clean them, to wash their feet.

Jesus knows everything, mind you. He knows what hell He was about to endure and go through. He could see the nails, the lashings, and the ridicule, and yet His final moments with friends should show us something about our suffering. While He suffered, He served. He wasn't holding a pity party or a bad attitude as to why He had to do this. He knew what He was made to do, and He would do it for us.

How? How could He know all of that and still grab a rag in a dimly lit room and clean His friends' feet? He knew the point all along was that this moment would forever be recorded in history for us to read. Not just to read, but to discover how we can go into our communities and schools and display true service. Service without the guarantee of promotion, platform, or payment.

True service is picking up the rags and getting to work. True service is loving your spouse. True service is helping a friend with their electric bill. True service is raising your kids in the way of the Lord and knowing that you're trying your best. We all have a rag, but the question for us is, will we choose to use it?

Will we choose to believe that the rag we hold is significant? Allow me to tell you that the rag you use is specific to you and your gifts, and people need your rag. You have a gift, and you need to serve people with that gift. Your gift was a gift from God to do what? To be a gift in service to those in this world.

It's on us to spread the gift through service. It's on us to bring hope to a hopeless existence and to be light in a dark society. We do that by spreading service, our specific service, to society and to people. This entire planet was and is forever changed through One man and His designated act of service to all of humanity, and now the invitation is to all of us here to spread our service to every individual we will ever meet. We will not be remembered by what we meant to do, but by the impact and influence we spread through this sphere.

5

Leading and Limping

We can lead in the face of what should disqualify us.

This might be news for you, or it might be old, but you have a limp. On your good days and your bad days, it's still there. It might flare up differently on your best day compared to your worst day, but it is inevitable, you have a limp. So do I. The beautiful thing about this limp is it makes you all the more real.

The limping means you're alive. The limping means you're here. If we didn't have a limp, we would not have the innate acknowledgment inside of us that we need help that only God can offer. Your limp was designed to show you that you can't do it on your own. Now, here is the kicker, the limp was placed into your life by the real modern-day circumstances around you.

Real with people, real with love, real with relationships, and real with yourself. What we often do, though, is we really try to hide our limp. To be completely open, trying to hide what is so visible never really works well. In a matter of time, you will be showing others your limp through decisions you and actions that do not run congruent with who you are. So, what's yours?

Before we get into a weird and bizarre limp comparison between our friends and peers, we really should define what the limp is. Our limp is not necessarily something we are born with but that which develops as we age. For example, in a previous chapter, we discovered that these horrible suicidal tendencies did not show up in my life until later. It goes deeper than that, though. Your limp comes from a past moment or trauma you experienced when you were younger.

I do not believe we were born to be alcoholic or drug addict. There isn't anything in me that believes that lie. What I do know is that your story had a rather unique experience as mine does. In those unique and often painful circumstances from our past, there is a rift created in our psyche, if you will. This created, for us, a hole. As you get older, you realize a young woman or young man needs the affection and accepting love of a father, and we can go into whole case studies of why the father figure is so important in today's world. Yet, your father left you, or your mother died, and that created for you a gap that you're still dealing with today.

For you, if you're a father, your family needs you. We cannot overstate that enough. You're the spiritual leader of those in your house, and God put them in your house to steward. Sadly, we as fathers are subject to the pressures around and within, and we still have to deal with our own limp as we watch our own children develop theirs. Yet, we must continue loving, leading, and living well. You can do this.

Hiding

Those games we would all play as kids had a lot of life to them, didn't they? Hide and Seek? King of the Hill? These were moments that meant a lot and made you come fully alive. At an older age, my brother introduced me to the world of shooting at each other with plastic balls filled with paint. Powered by some CO_2, these little pellets would fly and crash into your skin at demonic speeds.

Typically, when we went, I was cowering behind some debris or some barrier the whole game. Pain? No, thanks. Terrified? You best believe it. Did I enjoy this game of modern-day horror? Not in the least. One obvious limp you could even discover from my life is fear.

Jamie seemed to have no fear as we got older. He could and would do anything, and the consequence was not even something for him to consider. He just went with it. In all honesty, Jamie was fully alive out in the open while I was hiding. You will never experience the life God has for you in fear.

Fear has a way of pushing you into hiding, and there you'll stay until you're old or you get over that fear. God died for your fear, too. This life has too much to offer for you to stay afraid and hide. God will meet you in the middle of the fear and help you along the way, but you have to take the next step towards Him despite the fear. Courage is simply choosing to do what you're afraid of anyway.

Do it anyway. Go after it with your face set like flint. There's so much more for you to experience on the other side of that decision. Your decision matters today to conquer the fear of tomorrow. We can't see what the next twenty-four hours hold for you or me, so let's run to the horizon trusting and believing that God is on your side and He has all the help you need.

There might even be a subtle fear inside of you that you're afraid people will know the real you. That once the mask falls off, they won't love you for what they really see. Have you ever felt like an imposter? It's all right; God knows you even if you feel like people don't know you. He doesn't see an imposter either; He sees you. God, in all of His great might and wisdom, knows we are all like grass.

There's nothing in your life you need to hide or hide from. Mr. Skeleton hiding in your closest is not bigger than the love He has for you. We all have issues and hangups, yet we can be confident that God loves you all the more for it. God isn't surprised or appalled by what He witnesses you do each day. Grieved? Sure. We know that because God has so much more to give than that particular item has to offer you.

To be open, God is more grieved by your choice that is harming you instead of helping you than He is grieved by you. You're the object of His passion and obsession and the sinner He is drawn to, and the forgiven sin is the byproduct of who He is. Let's be honest, God is grieved not by you but by your sin. He came first and foremost for the lost, limping people—the cashier at your local grocery store and the well-educated entrepreneur in the seventh-floor conference room.

We all have had those shared yet different experiences from our past. Nobody has a perfect past. You are not your past, and you should not identify with your past. God came to redeem your past; He is going to use everything in your life, the good and the bad. He's the God of both. He is not disappointed in your past or your present.

Our limps come from a really dark place, if we are being honest. Yet God allowed it to happen to ultimately form you into the person He created you to be. He created you to lead and lead well. What can make that extremely difficult is your limp. Your limp can get in the way, right?

For example, your limp might be something called anger. You have been dealing with it for quite some time, and now it's here and unavoidable, and it's manifesting in your driving (road rage is real) and the sentences you speak to your colleagues or spouse. Hear me out, I am not a psychologist in the least. I just know that your limp came from something when you were younger, and now the question remains, will we deal with *it*, or will *it* deal with us?

Thorns

Paul in the Bible is a character we could all relate to on some level. He is first introduced as a character who is responsible for sentencing Christians to jail and flat-out murder. His limp was hate if we look at the story. He hated the early Christians, and he was out to get every last one, whether you relate to Paul on his limp, which could have been the utmost hate for those around him or in his transformation.

Paul gets knocked off his donkey and is given a revelation by Jesus to go to a destination and begin this brand new journey with Him, where he will be responsible for taking the Gospel to many people—on top of that, writing most of what we know as the New Testament. Paul goes from murderer to man of God in a heartbeat. Yet, he still had a limp.

In our story, he begins to plead for this limp, or in other words, this thorn, to be removed. We aren't sure what it is; all we know is it is affecting him. Are you being affected by this thorn that won't go away? Is the addiction winning? Are your selfish tendencies prevalent over your marriage? We have good news to discover together.

Through this narrative, we discover that God tells Paul that though he might have this thorn, we have a special grace to help deal with this thorn. God gives grace; in fact, God is grace. Grace is the unmerited, undeserved favor from heaven. Grace can be defined simply as getting what you did not deserve. That's Jesus.

We did not deserve Him, but there He is, ready to help us in our limps and thorns. The truth of the matter is that we have all grieved God more times than we can count, yet He stands at our door ready to go with us every single day. Your limp does not disqualify you from leading people, and in reality, speaking as a parent, makes God love you all the more. Where sin is, grace is there so much more.

Grace should be on every highway and byway in our languages and lives. Grace should be exercised in every relationship we carry, and we should do our best to exemplify this amazing grace from heaven. In another definition, we could define grace as empowerment—divine help from our Creator to use on this broken planet. There's a specific grace for you and your life.

What grace is not, though, is a license to use your limp as an excuse. You cannot use your limp as a crutch to use as a reason why you do what you do. We all have the option to change, and we can change. You can change. God creates us to change into His image, and ultimately that comes down to us and our own decisions. The greatest lie we believe is that we cannot change, but the greatest truth we have is that we can change. It's on you to be like Christ.

My mother smoked cigarettes for a lot of my young adolescence, and to be candid, I still enjoy the smell of them on the street or in passing cars. Does this mean it's good for me? Definitely not. This speaks to our thorns directly because it may feel good, but that doesn't mean it is good for you. You can change. You can be new in a moment with His power at work within you.

Today is the day that you begin to change yourself with His help and only with His help. This is not some self-help knowledge; this is the real God in flesh and bone who walked with us and talked with us and is readily available for you. Don't get it twisted, though; in your trial of changing yourself into His image, you cannot change people. We can't. It's impossible. When you do try (go ahead and attempt it), you'll end up frustrated and upset that they are not meeting your expectations of them.

Thank God for Jesus. We all had an expectation we could not meet in our lives, called sin, that really disrupted things. Yet God didn't force change on you; God is not a manipulator of people; He's the Master of the universe who sent Jesus to change us into what He had for us all along. The expectation was too high because of our shortcomings and failures, and God didn't compromise when He sent

Jesus for us; He conquered sin and defeated death, hell, and the grave so we could live past that expectation because of His work on the cross.

This is the good news for those who are reading these very words that there is a cure for your limp named Jesus. He just might not take it from you because He knows if it's in your life, the limp, it'll push you straight to Him. Let the limp lead you straight to Him, and there you will find the resolution and answer you have always been looking for. I have to warn you, though, the answer may not be entirely what you were hoping for.

Answers

There seems to be a response or an answer to everything under the sun these days. From modern-day technology to new vaccines on the horizon in the field of science, it seems we have more answers coming our way. What if the answer to your pain doesn't come? This is not bad news for us either; it actually breeds hope in that we will have an answer for our pain in eternity when we go home. On this side of mortality, though, what if we never know the reason for the pain?

In my early childhood, we would often travel to Florida

to see my grandparents. These were days filled with the warm sun, sandy toes, and countless hours of swimming and sunburn. Aloe is a gift from heaven. My grandfather was interesting in that he was a man of few words but so kind. Word of caution to parents of young children out there, just because they are kind doesn't mean they are of the utmost benefit to your children.

We didn't have a lot to be careful of, and my parents truly didn't have much of a reason to keep too much of a watchful eye present on us kids, but here is where complacency can cripple a child. My grandfather really had a limp and a lean towards women, and this was evident through the bathroom magazines he had handy (hello). If you know anything about lust, it's real, and it doesn't care what your first name is or where you're heading. It just wants you.

Lust has one motive and one desire: to ruin your plans and those around you. Lust is also developed in those dark spaces and places we don't let people inside until it's too late. It begins with thoughts, light and momentary. Next, it moves to daydreams and decisions, and lastly, it's bred in actions that cause pain—a lot of it. Lust doesn't care if you have a family or are trying for one; it slowly erodes everything around it until the affair has grown into full fruit.

My limp slowly and patiently began to develop at that fragile young age. I wish I could tell you I had the answers for why God would allow that kind of influence in my life at an early age. I don't. In all the books we have in the world today, I wish I could provide the answer to why your mom dealt with the dementia that ultimately led her to her grave. I don't. God really didn't offer us an answer; He offered us a Person who is the answer.

The incarnate God-Man would come down from heaven for you and me and experience every pain and trial we could ever even think of. This was to show everybody that He is the answer and lived to show us that. Allow me to show you what I mean. Jesus has the comfort that you need after you hit rock bottom. Jesus is the supply when all you see around you is lack. Jesus is the joy you've needed when the depression has caused your knees to buckle.

Life has a way of canceling all of our promises and hopes and dreams and leaving us with questions and doubts and concerns and a plethora of anxiety, but I can promise you one answer for your entire life while you live with your limp: Jesus. It's just Jesus. After the hurt, it's Jesus. After the addiction, it's Jesus. After the pain, it's Jesus. He's the answer for humanity, and He's readily available for you at this moment in time and space.

In all His ways, He is ever-present and ever ready to assist you and aid you as you traverse this limp that fell into your possession. Can I tell you that He isn't disappointed in your limp, either? He isn't angry with you; He isn't scathing with red hot anger towards you. He is near, and He is here. There's a particular passage that speaks about His desire for mercy and not sacrifice. His desire is for you to be with Him. With Him, you may not discover the answer, but you will discover His Person, and that is better than any answer the world wide web can provide.

6

Corrupted and Called

The calling ahead of you is greater
than the corruption within.

The Bible narrative is filled with so many applicable
and relatable stories. It speaks on our internal struggle,
it directs us on the way of wisdom, and the debate really
could be made in a definite for us on the defense side of
the court that those who live according to its principles and
statutes will come out with a better life and more satisfac-
tion. This does not mean you will attain everything you
have always wanted, and it does not promise you your way
to success. It just helps. One profound truth we are let in on
in an early story is of a king named Saul.

Saul was the result of a desperate plea by the people
who wanted a king instead of a God. Talk about wrong person and wrong answer. This is what comparison can do to
you; it'll give you answers you didn't know were the incor-
rect ones and leave you even more desperate. In this story,

the people of the day are looking to their right and to their left, and all they see is kings reigning and ruling the land all the while God, your God and mine, was leading them. Yet, that wasn't enough.

Enter Saul. If you will, Saul was the cream of the crop. The sharpest pencil in the drawer. The most colorful crayon in the box. You get what I mean. Yet, Saul, we would shortly discover, had a disobedience problem. The king they begged for couldn't even obey the God who put him there in the first place.

Notice with me though that order, God put Saul in charge by appointment of the prophet Samuel knowing full well that he would fail. We still have a problem named Saul in our society, and unfortunately, it starts with your first name and ends with your last name. We all have failed God more times than we can count, and yet, He puts us where He puts us.

To put this deeper, we all have a sin issue. Our Scripture explicitly tells you and me that we all have sin in our hearts, and sin corrupts. Sin has no benefits though it feels good at the moment. Sin is out to do one thing and one thing only, entice you to live the life God has not called you to live. Simply, to exist apart from the God who breathed the breath of life into you in the first place. This is what sin does.

Brace yourself because this is where it gets heavy for a few moments. Sin disrupts, sin invades, sin abolishes freedom, sin is a snare meant to squeeze the life out of you, and sin distracts. Your calling is too great to settle for the sin in front of you. Saul had an amazing future ahead of him, if we are being honest. The first ordained king for the people of God.

We will never know the alternative story of a God-fearing Saul who led the people well and didn't stray from the path of God. We will never see that because the story has already been written. Did you know that your story has already been written, too? God sees your whole life from outside of time but, in His power and might, He gave us something called free will. We make the choices. We make the decisions.

Now, the impetus of this whole book rests on the shoulders of God, who uses both our bad and great decisions. Yet, if we don't learn, it is possible to live a life He never called you to live. Allow me to explain. You're supposed to be living at such a greater capacity, yet you have settled for something so comfortable and convenient, and God will allow you to stay there. He isn't a puppeteer from heaven dangling ropes tied to manipulation in order to steer your life.

Have you gotten comfortable? Have you gotten so accustomed to your way of living you have forgotten what faith even is? Faith is the belief that God is steering my life towards the direction He has for me, even when I cannot see it. That's not comfortable. Sin makes you comfortable. Saul was comfy, if you will.

He was comfy making decisions apart from God, and that's when He started getting in trouble. From Saul's beginning to his end, we see a man who truly forgot to include God because of the corruption from within. Sin will steer your life in such a way where you have stopped including God in your daily decisions. Sin will make you think you can do it on your own. That's what Saul saw, and that's what led to his untimely demise.

Do you see how heavy sin is? Please note, though, Saul's destruction didn't start all bad; it just started with a decision. One decision after the next, and before he knew it, he was facing his death because he thought he could handle it all by himself, and the pride of life literally choked the life out of him. God allowed it to show the people that He is the one that they have always wanted and needed, and they failed to acknowledge time after time.

What decisions have you made that you forgot or even

neglected to include God in? I'm not saying you need to ask God what you're going to have for lunch today though I do believe fast food is from heaven. It's our modern-day manna. What I am saying is that your decisions matter immensely. The decisions you make today will most definitely impact and shape your tomorrow.

Sin is rooted in a deliberate act or decision. This might just be so applicable it sounds like I am coming off sarcastic, but I'm not; it's just truth: sin is a decision or lack thereof. Your decisions are counting on you. We must own the responsibility in our decisions and actions so we can become who He has called us to be in spite of the corruption that clings within. God made His decision long ago about you and your present predicament, and He is watching you and every decision you will make.

There's often a question that is thrown around in Christendom, "How do I know I'm in the will of God?" The answer is your decisions. Track them. Day by day and season by season, and I know they will be a great revealer of which track you are on: yours or His. Saul had one bad decision after the next, and this led to his tragic story we see unfold before our eyes in the biblical narrative.

That got heavy. Here's where your party can start again.

God still picked you. There isn't anything that disqualifies you from God resisting you and not choosing you. We discover through some ancient songs that God knew your days before you ever would, which means He knows the bad and the good, the prom night and the rejection. He knows you and all your skeletons in your closet and still chooses you a million times over.

He's the God of both. He knew the deliberate decisions you would make, and He knew who you would meet on that app that you had no business being on, and He is still in the business of redeeming people. There is no decision He cannot redeem and no moment in time that He can't work into a beautiful story. That's who He has always been, the Divine Storyteller who is telling story after story of grace and forgiveness of people who got stupid over time and action.

Saul was so bad in all of his decisions, and yet God still included him in the canon of Scripture. Why? Not to make a mockery of him but to show us here today of the detriment behind excluding God from your life. Now truly, we can't excommunicate God from our lives, that would be heresy, and we don't have that kind of power. But God can at times give you over to what you want more than Him so you can ultimately go back home.

Return

Here is where we are introduced to one of the greatest stories ever told. This story and this story alone would change everything for us. The biblical fatheads of the day, the Pharisees, knew basically everything about God, but they didn't know God. Be wary when your knowledge exceeds your intimacy of Him. We can get so smart in the day and age we live in due to the power at our fingertips in our screens and tablets, but we can miss Jesus. You might just be frustrated because you have missed Jesus and substituted the Son with product knowledge. Jesus isn't a product, He's a person, and He wants to be truly, intimately, known by you.

Jesus is in this story telling us the narrative of a father who had two sons. The younger son was ready to transition from the father and his property and go live his own life. In modern-day terms, what he was about to do, would be repulsive. He asks his father for his share of the inheritance. Inheritances are only given when there is a deceased individual present; here, he was not. He was surely alive.

Yet this son and all his entitlement goes to his father and basically tells him, "You're better off dead." Imagine that. Imagine that kind of grief from the father's end of the bargain. There wasn't anything in this deal to serve the father, only the son. This was not normal, and this was not acceptable, yet the father accepted it and gave him over to what he wanted.

Be watchful of what you want over God because, at that point, it's no longer a dream or a goal but a fallacy. As the story goes, the son runs and does what he wants to do with the father, nowhere to be seen. Here's where it gets dicey, any time you desire that object or position more than the Giver, you'll be left empty. If you're empty, it might be time for you to return.

God isn't up in heaven disappointed in your decisions and actions; He knew what you would do long before you knew what you would do. He is gracious and so compassionate. He doesn't need an explanation, and quite frankly, He just wants you. You are His obsession and prized possession. You are the only thing He died for.

Come back home, sinner. Though you are in the pig-pen like the son ends up, he has a realization. He smells. He is atrocious. He is covered in filth. Your decisions are not final; God's Word is. He has made up His mind about you, and nothing can change it. Abortion? You can go back home. Virginity lost? Go back home. Racist? Return home. Nobody is too far gone.

As the story goes, the son picks himself up and starts the journey home. We need to take note of the author of the story; it was and is Jesus. If Jesus spoke it, it can be done. With the authority from heaven, you can pick yourself up. God makes champions, and He makes conquerors. You have all the permission you need to return to the Father. Don't you dare allow anybody to speak anything else in your life.

We see the son on his way home, and we see the father waiting expectantly for the son. All the father needed was the slightest glimpse of the son for him to do something that was unacceptable in the day and age this oracle was spoken. He ran. Men didn't run. Yet this wasn't really just a man.

This was the most descriptive image that the God-Man named Jesus gave us of God the Father. He doesn't operate the way we expect Him to. He isn't predictable, and He isn't on our level. His thoughts and His ways are at a higher altitude than our comprehension. In other words, you haven't figured out God, and we won't. He's mysterious.

He calls the corrupted and doesn't apologize for it. At

this moment, the father runs and grasps and embraces the son and adorns him with the finest of clothing, and leads him back home, his original home. After his ridiculous and horrendous decision, he leads the son right up the steps, and I am sure no doubt opens the door for his son, who disrespected him to the highest degree. The best part? The pig would be slain for this return. They saved pigs of this size and weight for something special, and this son, who once was lost but now was found, was special to the father.

You're so special to God. He chooses to be there with you and for you every single day because He can't help it. He's drawn to you. He needed somebody to love, so He breathed the breath of life into Adam and had His first person to love. I think we need to be reminded, but out of the seven billion people on the planet now, and who knows what it was then, He would have walked that bloody path to Golgotha for just you.

The celebration takes place, but there is one individual that was not fond of this moment, the older brother. He was ticked. He didn't believe the son who ran was worthy of the love he was now receiving inside the house. God doesn't miss a thing. They have a conversation, the older son and the father, and lets him in on a profound truth. Everything that was the father's was his too.

God gave you everything. He equipped you for this life because He knew this world needed your influence, and He knew He could trust you as a carrier and vessel for His glory. King David mentioned something like this to us in that he never witnessed those God loved and chose to beg for bread. We don't have to beg God for anything in our lives; we just have to believe God. Belief is the hard part. How do we believe in a God who is invisible yet ever-present in our times of need? How do we believe in a God who accepts us in our shame and sin, and yet we have never seen Him in the flesh?

Believing is receiving what good things God has for you when you can't see Him, hear Him or feel Him. This is faith. Trusting in a God who loves me when I run and is there for me when I decide to go back home. Will He love me if I never return? Of course. Will this promise me eternal salvation? Depends on who is asking and who is writing the story. Can we give God the benefit of the doubt on who will be waiting for us in heaven?

Heaven will surprise us on who is actually there and who isn't. Heaven will reveal truly just how scandalous the love of the Father really is. The education inside the cranium writing these words to you is not smart enough to debate anybody on salvation; I just know that I have taken God at His Word, and when we discover that His mystery is greater than any wisdom from a human, we'll settle down a bit on these age-old arguments. All I know is that there is a return waiting for you and at the end of the return? The Father with his arms wide open.

Airports

To be honest, I love airports. If I could rent a three-bedroom studio in one, I would. The busyness of the airport matches the chaos in my mind, and for some reason, I just thrive in it. From the multitudes of people to the different experiences and food available, it's a people lover dream spot. Everybody is in a hurry somewhere. I've had the privilege to travel quite a bit and one story sticks out to me the most.

Right after high school, I had my escape plan, ready to take on the world. Mind you, this beautiful journey of following Jesus had not started yet. There were a few prominent government organizations that I had studied for my departure into adulthood, and then God had other plans. On my way home from a failed plan but a fulfilled call in Jesus, I was homeward bound again. Jesus had just wrecked my life in the best way possible, and the insatiable desire to read His Word overtook me. Yet, here I was, on my way back home after a failed venture out, and there was only one person waiting for me at the top of the escalator in that Atlanta Airport.

Dad. With arms wide open, he greeted me with a big bear hug and loved me right where I was at. God loves you right where you are, don't be an idiot like me and jump on a plane to figure that out. Out of the millions of people on this planet, He picked you for this life to live. This world is better and will always be different because of your unique thumbprint on it. Don't believe anything different.

No sin too great, no decision too grand, no mistake too big that God cannot forgive. He openly forgives. In His essence of who He is, is forgiveness, love, grace, mercy, and peace. Now, the decision is yours to truly forgive yourself as He forgave you and meet Him at the top of the escalator, waiting to embrace you as you make your return home. The truth is, we are all corrupted with sin, and that draws Him to us because He is obsessed with us and after us and never leaves us.

7

Victim and Victor

We aren't held hostage by our story anymore.

In all honesty, in my own life, I've played the "V" card way too much. Not virgin, the victim. There are moments in all of our stories where we were dealt the wrong hand, and nobody besides God will be able to better explain why your life played out the way it did. In reality, there's a wager I wouldn't mind putting money on (did he just mention gambling in this?). The wager is that even if we knew why what happened, happened, we would still be in our same position.

There's a lot we will never know on this side of eternity. Cancer is a great unknown. Car accidents can happen, and fatal ones at that, unemployment for drastically long seasons. Even if we knew the why behind it, we still could not change anything about it; do we wish it was different? Of course. As one preacher put it, "There's a lot I wouldn't have chosen but nothing I would change."

Can we look at life that way? I'm speaking on extreme ownership over your life and over my own. Ownership is what separates us from the victims. News flash, you are not called to be the victim forever. For a season? Quite possibly. We are all guilty of the pity parties we hold. There has to be a moment where you pull yourself from the ring as the referee is counting down to the knockout. Bloodied and beaten, you have to make the conscious decision to become the victor.

Your family is waiting on you to make that decision. Your kids are waiting on you to make that choice. Nobody else can make that decision for you. There must be a time where we take that decision and go after it, and we make up our minds to conquer the baggage within. It's okay to be angry, by the way. It's okay to be upset, to feel. These feelings are validated by your life, but here's where we should do some work; those feelings are keeping you from the life you have always been meant to live.

A lot of the trouble I got in in my early twenties was due to the fact that I didn't take ownership over my decisions or what had happened to me. Life is that way; it's not what happens to us but what we do with it when it happens. We all must take account of every page of our story, even as we turn this very page in a few moments. Life cannot guarantee you much, and we live by the promises of God, but I can tell you that the moment you start to take a look at your life and begin to connect the dots from bad to worse to great and good, we can have a new outlook on life and begin this journey of being a victor.

Baggage

Shortly after discovering Jesus' love for me and my life, I was hungry to go after Him. As you read in earlier chapters, we lived in a smaller town, and this chicken was ready to fly. There was an incredible church in the Pacific Northwest which had a world-class leadership program tied to Bible college, and I had just paid for my oneway ticket out of dodge. It felt surreal to pack everything I owned (literally) and get ready to head into the great unknown. There are moments we never forget, and if you have, it's time to try and remember.

Remembering ties the memory to your present-day circumstance, and there in that space, the groundwork can begin to become the victor. Let's just get over the fact that we have a hard time forgetting stuff. There's a reason for that. It will either breed gratitude or regret, and the decision is in your hands. Regret is the language of the victim, but gratitude is the dialect of the victor.

Do you want a great faith practice? Faith truly is a muscle, and this practice can build it. Go back over your life, all the horrid moments and the mountain highs, and write it all down. Write it all down to even this moment, reading this book. My prayer is that you'll discover that you're *here*. That you're alive and breathing and that oxygen is making its way through your veins and in your bloodstream.

Your brain is working at levels we still have a hard time figuring out how it does what it does. Your heart is pumping blood daily throughout your body. The skin on your body is shedding and making room for the new cells. After all the pain, trauma, and heartache, you're here. This is a promise to what is ahead of you. Playing the victim will keep you and your story cemented into the past.

Gratitude, the path of the victor, will keep you looking ahead to new events and people and places. You see, when I spent my two years in Seattle, most of me was still in Georgia. There were moments I was processing and building, and some memories I was learning how to tear down the stronghold. This led to days and weeks of being the victim over and over again. To be clear, this cost me.

The price was that I paid far too much in the present moment because the past was weighing me down. Are you weighed down by your past? Your past is passed now. You can look ahead to new and brighter days ahead. This can be your first day of believing in the good things that God has for you and rejecting the past mistakes. Do you feel as if you have messed up God's plan for your life? You're not that powerful.

We all have baggage. There is stuff that we all carry that makes us who we are. Now, back to that chicken that just wanted to fly. The morning I left, all I had was this old piece of luggage that was frankly big enough to carry a corpse and my backpack. Through the train that got me to the airport, through the airport and layovers, it was time for me to leave where I was with all the baggage I had. You're not all you are. You're that plus the baggage.

Every emotional experience, every memory and moment, all stored and archived in your back pocket called your brain. In a conversation I had recently, the pastor said, "Better to unpack now than when you're fifty." Man, that is potent. The moment you begin to unpack your baggage and take account of all your stuff is when breakthrough happens. We aren't supposed to go to our coffin as a victim.

The coffin is waiting for us at the end of all this, but it's up to us to get in it without regret and shame and guilt. Sadly, the dilemma we are all in is that of the victim mentality. Life is too short for you to be weighed down by that. We have to break free from this and live the journey we are all called to be on. To live free.

Baggage is heavy and quite obnoxious. Walking through the train to the airport was exhausting. Your baggage is hurting you until you take inventory of it and learn from it. There isn't a single piece of useless moments in your bank of memories; God is intentional. God is so intentional in that He allows for space and gives grace to you for this wrenching moment of learning what you want to keep and what you want to grow from.

Could it be that you're exhausted and weighed down by the internal baggage you're refusing to unpack? When I made it to the airport in Seattle, my bag didn't exactly come out the way I would have wanted it to. It came out of the receptor wide open. Invigorated with rage, grasping it with both hands, I ripped it off the conveyor belt and tried to close it. The zipper had broken (I'm telling you, this was older than Moses). For a moment, my mind played this reel in my head that the employees of the airline that were so dutifully diligent and responsible for my bags' safety and well-being had sifted through my stuff.

That was a hilarious thought as I realized what had actually happened. It's not so funny when we think that that is how people view you and your stuff. Can I be so bold in that people aren't caught up with your stuff but their own? We all have baggage that is wide open for the world to see, yet the only eyes on us are our own. This is good news because we can now build our focus on what we want to keep and what we want to throw out.

Now, this is crucial; whatever you decide you want to keep in your baggage will determine whether or not you become a victim in this moment or a victor. Each of us has experienced times and spaces in places that will either make us into the victor that we were created to be or a self-made victim. We can't afford any longer to hold onto those memories, and if we do, we need to change the view of them, and when we do, their power changes.

Are you ready for a power change? For a shift? To have different conversations with yourself? It's time to dump the baggage you've been holding on to for years. There's a safe place for them, too, at the foot of the cross. There are victors that have gone on ahead of you that have figured out the superior place of placing their stuff and dropping it at the foot of our bleeding Savior. Do you realize the importance and significance of Jesus?

Without Jesus, we have seven billion people or so on this planet with no hope and no chance of a future. We have all these souls playing victim and not one victor to look to. But thank God for Jesus (the Trinity explanation is for another time and a smarter guy). Jesus came down from heaven when we had no chance and no future ahead of us and created champions. He healed the lame and the leper. He opened the eyes of the blind and the deaf ears.

This is humanity's and heaven's Champion. Death was our destination, and the life of a victim was all that was there for us until Jesus stepped in. We need to take a moment and realize that if it wasn't for Jesus, we would not be where we are. There would be no blessing and no promise for us. Jesus is the world's victor, and He's ready to help you with the baggage that you have. The beckoning in front of you is greater than the burden behind you.

Conversations

Shortly after Jackie and I got engaged, we began the process of premarital counseling. If you haven't done this yet and you're close to marriage, allow me to strongly encourage you to do this. You're paired with another amazing couple in the church who have more years in the game than you do, and you go through some sort of book on marriage (surprise). Yet, in all of the chapters and the words, what was truly life-changing for our marriage was the conversations that surrounded the table for twelve weeks. Jackie and I had dug into our pasts a little bit through dating and the engagement, but nothing prepared us for this.

Conversations have a way of healing past hurt. The act of speaking and verbalizing the internal pain you have dealt with is freedom for your soul, and it releases you from your own shame, sin, and past regrets. It allows you to become the winner you were always supposed to be. Speaking breeds strength, and strength creates the spirit to keep on fighting in light of all the hard moments in life. What are you openly choosing not to speak about? What conversations are you avoiding?

There is a special and sacred thing that surrounds a table with friends you can trust where you just let it out.

Where you speak your mind, Christianity, in its essence, is spread through conversations around a Creator God who was formed in flesh and bone and lived with us. Your perspective can shift in a moment from one conversation.

Why do you think therapy is so effective? Because it's one person or party openly describing and speaking the issues happening underneath. You can share what is going on. You can let it all out at the coffee shop or on the car ride. You may, in fact, be a completely different person on the other side of it, and this entire moment was waiting on you to speak. I'm just going to put it out there; we cannot afford to stay silent on our problems and issues.

They grow in the dark of our minds, but when we start the dialogue, the light shines in. Mental illness is rampaging through our populations and cities and urban neighborhoods, and could it be tied to the fact that we feel more alone than we ever have? Could it be our texts have replaced something of more value? Could it be our screen time is causing us to sour while our lips can produce life?

It may be time for you to find a trusted friend or go to your spouse or even your pastor if you have one and unload everything. Even the crumbs at the bottom of the backpack need to be taken out. You have never felt better than when you have confessed to the internal conflict. Why do you think conversations with Jesus changed people? The amazing and incredible aspect of this is we can still go to Jesus, and there He'll be waiting for us with His classic saying, "Do you want to be well?"

Well, do you? We can shift and change in a moment and over the course of many moments when we have dialogues with those who are closest to us about what is going on. We cannot wait any longer, the Savior is calling us, and His call equips us to be the victors we were always supposed to be.

8

Stirred and Shaken

The world needs stirred people.

As I write this, I'm sipping my cold brew coffee (the only real coffee) in a campsite with no cell service around. My family is asleep, and all around is the silence of the hills here in the great state of California. The brisk morning air is biting at my skin, but overall, there is only peace. Peace we haven't seen in a while, if we are being candid. Over these last few weeks, we have seen a country fall within itself, and we've witnessed the horrors of earthquakes, flooding, death, and disease. The worldwide pause we experienced in 2020 seems to be in a continuation, and the economy doesn't look too bright. Weeks prior to this, we had the chance to say goodbye to a loved one who would then swiftly pass away from cancer. Life doesn't seem on the up and up.

If we aren't careful, we really can be challenged in our faith. Challenges, though, are a great and indicative look into the authenticity of your faith and my own. What do we do in a world where it feels like God is silent and we are left to deal with our own state? We get shaken. The shaking is paralyzing and hard to look past.

Simply, the shaking is messing with us. We all feel like birds in cages, and the events around us are rattling the cages we are in. These are very real circumstances. This is very real pain. In looking back, though, we can see these same events, different in our day and age but nonetheless the same, transpire in the biblical narrative. The Bible wasn't meant to be just read but lived out in practice.

God is very intentional, and there is a specific reason He gave us His Holy Book. To inspire, to change, to provoke, to challenge, to bless, and to show us Jesus. At the time, the orators and the people who wrote the story were experiencing death, destruction, violence, upheaval, and pain. Yet hope came from all of that. It's been the most attacked and ridiculed book in history because we can't get our minds completely around it.

What do we do when we can't get familiar with something? We fear it and reject it. What if you stopped fearing the Bible your dad read, and you started to read it on your own? What if you started to develop your own faith? You would be shocked and utterly surprised at what the Bible really is about. From the world then to the world now, we are experiencing the same pain, just different events.

The blessed truth we have in our tool belts is that this book is living and breathing and true, and it'll be here for us in moments that get dark such as this hour in humanity. The Bible is about One person, and that's Jesus. Jesus showed up in the darkest hour for humanity after hundreds of years of silence. Between the Old Testament to the New, that small gap was filled with only silence. We do not have anything recorded from the lips of heaven.

In the silence we are feeling today, could it be a setup for the greatest arrival of revival that we have ever seen? We may not know until it's here, but I'm stirred to believe that. Our world today needs fellow humans who are no longer shaken but stirred. Shaken people produce anxiety but stirred people produce praise and prayer. The sweet tea we all loved in the suburbs of Georgia was not sweetened until it was stirred. This is the scene for us of the disciples in the upper room.

The disciples and followers of Jesus just experienced

the pain of a lifetime from the Man who claimed to be God yet was dead in the flesh. We know they were afraid, shaken, by the horrific events that had just transpired in front of them, and now they are hiding. Shaking will do that to us. We can't control anything, so we try to control what we think we can: ourselves. So they hid.

While they were hiding, though, a stirring was about to happen. As we read the narrative, a high and mighty wind came in with power, and they began to be filled with this power. Power came to them as they gathered together with one purpose and in one accord. This power created in them the stirring and the movement we know as the church today started. Stirred people stir people, and the opposite is also true; shaken people can shake people.

As believers in the global body of Christ, we can stir people up. We can stir them up by our praise of the One who died for us and came back from that tomb. He's the only one in humanity who predicted His death, burial, and resurrection. That stirs me. Because that stirs me, it can stir you too. Can you imagine one local body after one local body stirred into prayer and praise of the One who loves us to the end?

There wouldn't be any more room for shaken people

and shaken media and shaken news. God isn't shaken, by the way. He isn't panicking up in heaven nor in our hearts. He knows exactly what He is doing in your life and in my own. That gives me assurance. Did the divorce papers just slide across the table from you? Did the prognosis come back in a manner you weren't hoping for?

God is present, and He's near, and He's in control, and He knows what to do and when to do it. Our unfortunate predicament is that we don't know when He will do it or how. Can I encourage you to be stirred instead of shaken? Your shaking is hurting you, and it's causing other people to be shaken too. The stirring is healthy, and it's filled with expectation.

Tides

Growing up, we lived in a houseboat for a temporary season. We were docked on a beautiful lake in Georgia, and I was only elementary in age. This created for us the unfortunate predicament of walking up the dock to the minivan in the cold and breezy mornings of winter. Dressed in the warmest clothes we had, my brother, sister, and I marched up the dock with our backpacks and lunches in hand. When I say cold, it was cold, and the dock was moving under the wake of the lake. The foundation was shaken.

We only had one option, to move forward to the promise of heat in the minivan. You really have only one option, forward. Victory is forward; the stirring is forward; the hope is forward. God is always thinking forward in motion. He has a plan, His plan, you know. The world feels like that dock in Georgia, moving and shifting while we are trying to cope with taking a single step.

Nobody won their fight by moving backward. We won't be remembered by our steps backward but by the leaps we took forward.

Moses felt that way. Charged with leading the entire nation of God's people, he himself was staring at the face of an impossible situation. The sea in front of him, the raging and violent army behind him. Up until this moment, forward still didn't even feel an option. Moses was stuck in the middle.

Do you feel like that? Stuck in the middle of the future anxieties and past pressures? We can take note of what happens next for us in this story. After a brief conversation with God, Moses knew what to do. Notice the flow here, though; it wasn't until after Moses inquired of God that he knew what to do and was stirred into action.

Prayer is a great prerequisite to the stirring in your life. When was the last time you let out a heartfelt and honest prayer to the One who made you? Often I have discovered that the sliver of difference between being shaken and stirred is honesty after all. All prayer is a dialogue between you and your Maker. Prayer is healthy; pride is harmful. We don't pray because we are too busy or because we fail to admit we need the help. This story would be rather ridiculous if Moses was too prideful to have this dialogue with God.

We are never called to panic, but we are shown how to pray. Prayer is the acknowledgment that God is in control and we are not Him. Prayer takes the focus off of our panic and onto His Person. Your panicking isn't doing you any favors but raising your blood pressure. Moses was given clear direction after the prayer, and this might be the season where you begin to raise your voice.

Once he realized what he needed to do, he did it. He raised his staff over the sea, and the tide split wide. They were in forwarding motion again, away from the chaos behind them. Stirred people look ahead to the future, and shaken people can only see the sea in front and the evil behind. Stirred people take other people with them, while shaken people bring people down with them.

This world doesn't need another single shaken individual, but a mass of people stirred together by one mind and one accord, knowing and trusting that God has it all together. God knows what He is doing, and we must take great confidence in that, even when we don't see it, feel it or hear it. God has a way of keeping us on our tiptoes right up until He shows up in all of His glory. He did it for Moses. He'll do it for you.

Here is some great news for us, too, especially if you find yourself in the shaking today. You can change. We saw this with Moses years earlier when he saw one of the locals being beaten by an Egyptian. Shaken people try to put matters into their own hands, as did he. As the story goes, Moses does the unthinkable and murders the man, and this is how we know he's shaken by what he has seen.

In a rapid turn of events, he hides the body and flees. Shaken people run while stirred people stay. Stirred people stare in the face of trials and hardships and believe God will show up. They expect God to appear on their behalf. Shaken people run and hide and wait until it blows over. Stirred people commit the matter to God's hand, while shaken people keep it in their own hands, thinking they can control the situation.

That's really it, though, isn't it? We love control. We desire to control how each day unfolds, so we set our alarms to control the way we wake up, and we control the coffee pot or French press to make us that morning caffeine kick. We proceed to the shower and control the water temperature to our liking, and we control the socks as they go on our feet.

Do you see how much we love control when in reality, the only thing we control truly is our attitude? We can't control this world and the plight of humanity. We don't know how this all comes to an end. We don't know when or who the next war will be with. Stirred people are good with no control, though, because we know Who controls all of this.

Jesus controlled the story. Who can say what He said without controlling the outcome? He willingly laid down His life; nobody took it from Him. Jesus was stirred in love for us and walked that hard path to Golgotha because He couldn't stand the shaking sin it had been done to His creation which was separation. We were all separated at one point in time, but by the cross, we are brought near, and because we are brought near, we ourselves are stirred and no longer shaken by the state of the world.

Anxiety

When we all get to heaven, part of me cannot wait to play the reel of why God put me in my chaotic family. There's truth for you in there, though. He put you in your family to turn that family around, and He's empowered and equipped you to do it. No matter how messed up or jacked up your family is or even appears to be, you can turn it around. Have you ever taken a look at the genealogy of Jesus? It's filled with people that made huge mistakes.

I'm by no means a pharmacist, but I am sure my dad's had a heyday with how much medication he would have to write for him to keep his anxiety at bay. Did it help? I'm positive. Was it beneficial? It could be argued thoroughly. Please hear me here; you are not weak for having a prescription; you're human. We are all like dust.

There are some generational items we are born into and some products we fall into. God can take care of both. He is about fixing people and fixing bloodlines and creating order out of chaos. I saw this at play in my own life.

Time and time again, I'd witness the subtle interaction between my parents as they would have a conversation around bills, payments, and finances, all the while the orange pill bottle would come about, almost like a Band-Aid for your permanent issue. In retrospect, God's hand has always been on me and you. There were some conversations I had with God at an early age, and one was that I never would take part in that. This is not a knock on you and your prescription; this is a conviction that was ingrained in me from childhood. Only God can take responsibility for that.

God has taken full legal responsibility for you and your life. He made it. He formed you and molded you and placed you where you are right now with the last name you have for a purpose, and that is to turn it all around with His help. It may have fallen into your lap, but with His help, you can manage it completely. Does it mean you'll be perfect? Far from it. God doesn't make perfect people, we have sinned, and we've all fallen short, and that's where His grace comes into action for you and me.

Now, with full disclosure, this means your parents weren't perfect either. That means I'm not perfect. Though I'd like to think I am, I'm not. My dad wasn't perfect either. Welcome to my life.

In high school, I worked as a bookkeeper at a local grocery store, and there I could credit a lot of my love for all kinds of people. From African American to Asian, we would see all of it, and I was right at home there. God is so intentional; I hope you know that. One particular night, I had the worst of chest pains. There were a lot of momentary pains, and I was shaken by all of them.

If you deal with anxiety on any level, you know what I am talking about—the shortness of breath, the tightened chest cavity, the clammy hands. In a swift phone call, I did what any son would do when he is in need: I called home. Queue the drive home and what my dad had in mind to help me. Reminder, not the best parenting advice, and now I can look back on it and laugh.

As we read earlier, we aren't perfect, and sometimes, the shaking occurring in your life will rock you to your core. It did for me. I pulled in, ran inside, and my dad handed me a fraction of the dose that he was used to taking all these years. In a matter of moments, I was out like a light. This story is for you to know that you might have messed up, you might have failed, you might have screwed up so bad either as a parent or as a son or daughter; there's still so much grace for you.

We can all come together and wholeheartedly admit we need the power of a resurrected Savior who loves us and died for us, and by His shed blood, we have the power to break anything shaking in our lives and be set free. Are you shaken today? Take heart in the living God who can bring your situation to a calm and stillness while changing that same emotion to being stirred. He's stirring you at this moment. He's moving in you at this moment, and He's going to stir you the rest of your life.

Accidents

Shortly after we got pregnant with Charlotte, life threw a curveball at us. My wife worked about thirty minutes from the freeway, and as we always did, we were having a conversation by phone call. Laughing and joking usually persisted throughout the banter back and forth up until a loud "crunch" took over the phone.

"Somebody just hit me," Jackie anxiously muttered to me on the phone.

As fast I could manage, I tracked her location by her phone and pulled up to the scene. They had her in the ambulance by the time I arrived, and for some safety measures, the paramedics had informed me they just wanted to be safe and take her into the hospital to see how Charlotte was doing. If you've read anything so far, you know Charlotte was born, and she turned out fine besides her awful attitude problem. What we weren't ready for were the next two weeks and the same exact predicament.

Jackie got hit, again, on the freeway. This time though, she was shaken internally. She was shaken by the trauma of both accidents, and she felt like she didn't have the power to continue on. When you're shaken by life and its events, it can do that to you. You can succumb to the things that have transpired, and you can feel afraid and scared.

It takes a stirred person to snap you out of it. It takes a stirred person to tell you, "We are getting through this together." Phone call after call, I had to engage with my wife and speak with the authority imparted to me from our Savior and tell her she could do this. You can do this, too. No hardship or event is stronger than His blood that is for you and with you and equips you for this life. We are told that the mind and spirit we are given are that of power, love, and self-control.

You have power. You have love. You have the self-control. We have all we need to become stirred for one another, for our families, and for our country, and we can move in the face of any accidents or horrors we are faced with. The world has never needed more stirred people who are moved with compassion, grace, patience, and mercy towards humanity. We are the only light this world has got, and we have the message of hope to all who have ears to hear. So let's speak without apology, and let's love without fear and go into our Monday stirred to stir people around us.

9

Raining and Reigning

He's above it all.

Let's keep this one short. In an earlier chapter, we had discovered together that the rain had gotten loud outside. Internally our minds are a mess, and externally, the world-wide economy seems to be fragile and brittle. Everywhere we look, we are struggling, and there are struggling people striving to just get by and survive. We may not see the other side of all of this right now, but we can trust that God sees both sides. We can believe He knows what is going on in the world today.

God knows why nations are in unrest, and He is aware of the racism and division in our very own country. He's using all of it, too. Not one event, not one drop of the rain is outside of His reign. He reigns above it all, and He's ever-present through it all. God is writing this story of our lives, not the news and not the critic. When you and I decide to believe that God is on both sides of this, it builds our faith and gives us hope.

Let's be honest, what is the alternative? To believe that He isn't in control? To believe that He isn't near? That breeds insecurity and cynicism. It takes faith to lift our eyes and our perspective and believe that He has all this chaos under control.

The reality is that it takes faith that God is who He is and that He is on both sides of your story, working every detail into it into a masterpiece. He's a creator; we discover that in the very beginning of our biblical narrative, and He still creates today. He's just using people and their stories to craft something for His glory. Do you feel like you've wasted time? Made some horrible mistakes?

He reigns. He's using all of it. He hasn't missed a detail of your life. How can it be that the God who reigns over the earth is closer than our next heartbeat? How can it be that after the abortion, He multiplied the babies in your womb and gave you everything you ever wanted, but you just didn't realize it yet?

How can it be that He stopped the disease in your blood only to use you to minister and speak to somebody else in your neighborhood who is dealing with what you dealt with? It's incredible. God uses everything. He uses all our mistakes, mishaps, victories, and celebrations as the tapestry around our lives.

What do we do with all the noise outside, though? Everywhere we look, there's something new to report that induces anxiety and stress on levels we can't even begin to comprehend. This might be so simple that it's offensive, but we choose to let it go. We let go of the stress that has been keeping us up all night. We rid ourselves of the anxiety that creeps up on you after lunch. Simply? We turn it off, and we turn to Jesus.

Our turning signifies that we aren't in control, that we don't reign over this worldwide kingdom. We don't have a say, but we can pray. The only thing we can control (most of the time) is our tongue, so we use it to pray. While we are struggling with the rain, we can often forget the power of prayer. You know God hears your cries, right?

He can hear the faintest cry. Allow me to show you. Jesus had just fallen asleep in the hull of the boat as the disciples manned the boat when torrential rain began. Not just any ran, ridiculous rain. The boat was breaking under the barrage of wind, rain, and waves. Hope seemed lost.

Peter, my favorite disciple because I relate to him on so many levels, goes to the only Person he can think of at the moment. The narrative goes that Peter woke Jesus with his plea. Do you think Peter's voice was higher than the breaking boards and roaring waves? Do you think Peter had that vocal capacity to do so?

Jesus heard his cry. Jesus has heard your prayer. He's on His way to answer it, but it may not be in the form or fashion of your preference. It's because He knows what is best for you and me. Do you believe that? He has your best interest in mind, and He knows how to answer it.

Rejection

To be honest, I wish I had this perspective fresh out of my short Bible college experience. We just moved to Jackie's hometown, and I needed a job. I applied at the first credit union I could find, and they hired me. This was not the end goal either. Ministry has always been at the forefront of my mind, and it doesn't let up.

Unfortunately, in ministry or not in ministry, you are guaranteed difficult people. People who look like you and talk like you and maybe even hold the same values as you do but are difficult. The perfect storm? When it's management in customer service. All this time at the credit union, I didn't realize that God reigns above it all. He knew what

He was doing with the difficult people around me.

Simply put, He was preparing me for what He had prepared for me—the same for you. You may not see the end result right now, but you cannot stop with difficult people or inconvenient jobs. God is using all of it to build you into who you are becoming. Little by little, day by day, He's up to something, and He doesn't waste any of it.

When I worked at the credit union, I always erred on the side of "get me out of here." So I did what I knew how to do, resume after resume and job application after job application. After a few interviews, it was the same response, "We've gone with another option." Rejection stings. It hurts.

For a while, it hurt, and after the hurt, I began to believe the lie that maybe I was meant to do only what I was doing. It only takes a little while for rejection to pry its way into your persona, and you start to believe lies that were never even spoken in the first place. I'm thankful today that God doesn't reject us, He approves of us and loves us, and He reigns through us and over us. He's in control.

You see, through this time, I was in my early stages

of communicating the Bible to elementary-aged kids, and all the while I was working them through their elementary faith, He was working in me the greater maturity to break out of my elementary faith. Elementary faith is believing He isn't with me because life is hard. It's acknowledging that because life is hard or we had a day that He isn't in love with us and has forgotten us. It's maturity He is after, and He often develops our maturity in the soil of rejection.

God didn't promise us a perfect outcome, but He did promise us His presence, and that is all we need to go into this life. Or even your Monday meeting tomorrow. His presence is what led the Israelites through the desert in the night and in the day. Can you believe that? The God of all creation was evident by day and present at night.

He may not appear in a plume of fire today, but He does appear through the kind word of a stranger, and even our Bibles say we may be entertaining angels. We can know that in the midst of the pain and hardship, He's present and near. He is at the bottom of the valley, and He's at the top of the mountain. He's everywhere, and He's got the whole wide world in His hands.

10

Dreaming and Drowning

God loves dreams, dreaming, and dreamers.

Somewhere along the way of life, I'd love to figure out where we lost our imagination. Do you remember having a wild imagination as a kid? Now what? It's turned to anxiety. We can hypothesize that we lost it between our first mortgage and junior high.

As a father to a toddler, it's been refreshing to witness the pure imagination of a child. No matter where Charlotte may be, she has imagination. She is dancing with no care in the world and no opinion of those who are watching her. After enough plastic cake going around, you could almost be convinced that she has eaten the delicacy of the pastry itself. She just imagines stuff. For example, the first thing I witnessed as I woke up this morning was her attempt at a song that is mildly annoying at this time in my life. The song wasn't even on. I'm so close to banning every platform known to mankind in my home so I can stop seeing these dance moves.

Certainly, we shouldn't have tea parties if we are above the appropriate age; that would just be ridiculous and creepy. But, we can dream. We can dream for a better life; we can dream and be inspired to gain our dream job or most ideal annual salary. In fact, there isn't anything unhealthy with dreaming as long as it's in accordance with God and His plan for you and not your own selfish desires. For example, if you're single and dreaming of marriage, you dream for that one person and not multiple. That's downright insane.

Dreaming can truly keep you afloat if you allow it to. Dreaming and envisioning the future empowers you to lift your head above the waters right now, and it helps you see the island not too far off. Of course, it's going to take some work and some swimming to get there, but the view of the island makes a world of difference. When you can see the destination, it propels you forward from your present loca-tion. One advantage that we can gain from drowning (albeit morbid perspective) is you're clinging and crawling to the surface.

What is it? You're looking up. Dreamers constantly look up and out toward the horizon. We've forgotten how to look up today. Leaders have forgotten how to shift their own perspective and look vertical. What's going on? We've shifted from vertical to horizontal and become fixated on our fellow man or woman who is dreaming, and we think to ourselves, "Only if I had the money, time, will, etc." The fastest way to pause your dream or prolong the start date is with that excuse.

Faith is a language free of excuses, and it's full of anticipation that God will come through for you while you dream and plan and envision. We've gotten caught up in a lot of excuses and forgotten how to take ownership over our lives and our current situations, which has left us drowning and gasping for air. Taking ownership will cause you to lift your eyes and your head and move onward.

Jesus anticipated the cross and the pain and the unfair trial. In His anticipation, He saw Jerusalem on the horizon for His whole life. He knew exactly where He was going and why He was going there. Every crowd was intentional, every conversation was deliberate, and above all, His eyes fixed on Jerusalem and those city gates He would walk through one last time as He went to the cross to die a death that was for us. Yet Jesus was dreaming of the cross. This was why He was here in the first place. He anticipated all of it.

Do you feel like you have been lacking anticipation? Do you feel as if nothing good is coming your way? Do you feel like you've been grasping for the surface for some time now, and you just can't catch a break? God has a way of breaking through at just the right time. For you and your dream.

From what we have read in our Bibles, God has a way of showing up in the middle of the paralysis. The world felt paralyzed in silence as creation groaned for its Master to come to its rescue, and God came in at just the right moment when Jesus came down as a baby in that small village manger. Everything the world anticipated for hundreds of years came in the form of an infant's cry. There's a holy reason God came down in the form of a baby to a virgin named Mary; because children know when to anticipate and how to do it.

Jesus was on to something when He mentioned to us that the kingdom of heaven would be for those who had childlike faith. Children dream. Children know where their help comes from. Children don't spend hours upon hours panicking over where their next meal will come from. They just trust and know that the parent will take care of them while they dream up dinosaurs and treasure hunts.

We can recapture that sense of imagination, but the truth is most of us are drowning. Not literally, I mean, you're reading this book. You're drowning in debt, you're drowning in fear, you're drowning in the thought of the unknown, and when you're drowning, it's hard to dream. God can revive even the most dead of dreams in the worst of circumstances.

What we are describing is the mere will to survive. You weren't meant to just survive and exist. That is not the definition of life and life to the full that Jesus taught. Jesus didn't die for you to settle in mediocrity and pay the mortgage and go to dinner once a week. He died for you to dream again, to live inspired by His life, and above all, to serve others.

Joseph knew this. At a young age, we discover that he had dreams, and he was hated by his brothers for it. You're going to be hated. Chances are, you're going to be disliked by even those closest to you. That's not on you to worry about. The greatest discredit to God would be paying attention to those people next to you while you forfeit the dream He placed inside of you. Don't settle to be liked and loved while your dreams are never pursued after.

This world needs you and your dream. This place is better because of your dream. Whether it's a career shift or a new hobby, it's there for a reason. Your dream is bigger than you think it is, too. You see, Joseph ended up saving his entire family through the God-given dream that was placed inside of him.

In this whole story, what does it have to do with you? While Joseph was drowning in prison, he never gave up on the vision that God placed inside of him. He still dreamed. I don't know the disappointments and upsets you have faced, but you cannot stop at the prison of inconvenience. Without the trouble, there wouldn't be the testimony. No hardship, no story.

There is a lot I can't guarantee for you, but one promise that is sure is there will be problems. In spite of the pain, God will use it. In light of the struggle, God will come through. In view of the anxiety, God will make a way.

You may be reading this and ready to settle for the mediocre and the "easy," path but nobody of significance ever stopped short. You're significant; you're unique; you're special, so you must not stop when the going gets tough. There's a lot of life ahead of you, and your dream is waiting for you, and by the way, you didn't just think up that dream.

God put it there in full view of the hardships you would face. He saw the addiction you would deal with, He saw the family member pass away, He saw the job loss and the financial ruin, but He allowed it because He knows you can overcome. He knows you are stronger than you think you are. This life is a race, and we can't give up when we're tired.

Nobody speaks about the champion who lost because he got too tired; they speak about the story of the winner who in spite of all his exhaustion and all his pain, continued and pushed through and won the race. This is for the mother on the brink of giving up. This is for the son who is ready to quit on everything that life has to offer. You can keep going, no matter the weariness you're presently feeling in this moment.

Exhaustion

Hawaii is one of my favorite vacations because it carries some of my fondest memories when life wasn't so chaotic in our family. Most recently, we had the privilege of going while Charlotte was only six months of age. With full expectation that it would be fun, we went. My wife was anticipative because it was her first time there, and I was ready to show her the sights. Then came Tuesday.

Have you ever had a day where it all changed in a moment? You had these dreams and these plans, then it all changed? The dream for me was to show her the sights and the views. Culture in Hawaii is beautiful, and I was going to show her until heat exhaustion got the best of me, literally.

Now you must know, nothing really keeps me down. Our motto when I was coming of age was that we didn't go to the doctor nor the hospital. My parents actually bred fear in us kids towards the hospital. So as you might expect, I was petrified when I was experiencing this level of weariness and tiredness. Yes, I do plan on paying for therapy in the very near future.

We had a full day ahead of us, and I could barely get out of bed. Nothing was lifting my strength, so we did what we had to: sent my wife and daughter to go enjoy the day I dreamed of while I lay in bed recovering. Tuesday was not my day. I'm assuming you know where this is going, but I'll make it clear. Tuesday was out of my control.

There will be a lot of events that take place in your life that you do not have control over. Bills will come, and the finances won't. Fear will come, and courage may not be present. You will come to the end of yourself and find yourself tired. Life has a way of beating you down.

Are you exhausted? Weary? Worried sick? Heartbroken? Do you feel as if you can't go another day in this chaotic mess called modern-day society? It's all right. Give yourself space to breathe and cope and to relax. This is something called self-care.

Self-care is not selfish, either. You may need to book that vacation that you're holding off on schedule. It's a very hard thing to dream while you're drowning, so it may be time to take hold of that buoy and rest awhile. While you rest, pray. While you rest, seek.

In the hotel room, while my best friend and daughter went to the island to explore, I rested, but I did not waste the time afforded to me. I podcasted. I prayed. I sought God's face while my face was in the pillow. Can I tell you that God ministered in that place? God was so present while I felt so exhausted.

Typically we don't experience the fullness of God's presence until we are lying down with no strength left, and we don't have to do that. God isn't waiting for you to experience a wake-up call for you to experience Him today. He's readily available now; He's accessible now. He's nearer than your next breath, and He's more than ready to be there for you in your point of exhaustion. But while you are exhausted, this is not your time to quit.

There was a moment where I needed to get out of my hotel room and feel the air I spent a lot of money to enjoy. Could I even walk? Barely. As I made my way to the elevator and down the lobby and onto the streets of Oahu, I needed some sort of food.

Thank God for those easily available and accessible convenience stores located on every square block. Just barely squeezing through the aisles to get some liquid in me to replenish electrolytes and some snack that seemed somewhat delightful, it was time to head back to the room. The point in this story? You can't die where you're exhausted. You must keep walking and keep pushing and pressing into your future.

The graveyard of unseen dreams is a big place, and we will never truly see the size and the depth of the dead dreams there. Dreams are susceptible to die in exhaustion, so we must pay attention to how we are doing on the inside to keep these dreams nurtured and fed. Have you heard of the story for parents on a plane? It basically summarizes that we as parents put the oxygen masks on first, and then we aid our child.

It may be time to take hold of that mask for yourself and catch some air. Nobody is in control of your present circumstance, but you and your family need you. Your community needs you. It's on you to heal and to gather the air you need to breathe to fuel that dream. This is where a lot of us go wrong in that we expect our spouse to give us the air we need or the manager at your employment to assist you in your walk, but most of the time, it's just me, myself, and I.

Let it be for us here, wherever you're reading this, going after your dreams, all the while finding spaces and places to rest along the way. Can God still allow you to dream while you're drowning? Of course, He's God. Joseph held onto God in the prison where he was wrongly imprisoned, and we can hold on to God while we feel under the weight of all the stress, pressure, and anxiety. Here's something we can take from this, God believes in your dream more than you do.

He's the one that put it there in the first place, and He's the one that will see to it. Paul wrote to us today that God will finish that which He starts. You may have started the dream or the non-profit or the church, but it was in God's mind before it was in your hands. This goes for everything in our lives, too. Your family, the one you prayed for, was in His hands before it was placed in yours.

God trusts you with what He gave you, so don't waste it. God didn't die for you to have your dream die due to exhaustion and pain and the stress and because life got too hard. He shed His blood for us so that in the middle of the pain, we would dream and work all the more towards what He birthed inside of us. This is called grace. Grace is the empowerment to do what you're here to do.

Do you feel as if your dream has slipped through your hands? Do you feel as if your aspirations have all sank to the bottom of this crazy season we've been in? It may be time to look at and experience the grace He has for you, which is unlimited. There's grace for your Tuesday and grace for your Sunday evening. Grace will allow you to operate in a capacity that is beyond your natural capability.

Grace will push you to what God has for you. It will lift your head when you're down and when you're clinging for air as you sink and you feel like you're drowning. Grace will be there for you as you go into what God planned for you, and here's the kicker, you cannot do it without His grace. Grace is the fuel for the vehicle you're riding in that will eventually get you to where you're heading.

Samaritan

Jesus was and is a great storyteller. He's God. He writes stories using illustrated sermons with our very own lives. We are His story, after all. He died for humans. He died for the whole world, and He's going to use us to share that story in the globe today. Even if we are silent, Jesus said the rocks would grow teeth, lips, and tongues and speak His story. That's terrifying if you ask me; let's stick with our own lips.

One parable Jesus spoke to us was about a man whom we don't even get his name. All we know is he is walking along on his own journey to somewhere, and he's confronted by thieves who beat him half to death. Life really can feel that way for us. We are going one way, and then we receive the phone call or text that changes everything. God saw it.

God saw the abuse in your childhood; God saw the heart attack that took your spouse; God saw the cancer that has now crippled your body. He didn't author it, but He will use it. This whole journey we have been on in this narrative is to discover that through your limping, your sin, our pain, and my fears is that God will use all of it. He's about to show us that.

We discover in this parable a man whose name is unknown to us and is bleeding and dying on the side of the road. He is passed by in this tragic story by people whom society has deemed important. God doesn't call people important like we call people important. He has a way of choosing the least of us to inspire the whole lot of us. As the story goes, this man's only hope while he's down and out is that of this good samaritan.

He patches him up, nourishes him a bit, gets him up on his way, and sends him to an inn. The inn was his place to rest and to heal, and the best news? This man paid the bill for the man to heal. News flash, you and I are not the good samaritan in this story; we are the man left for dead on the side of the road.

People may have passed you by and left you for dead in your dreams, but God will never leave you for dead. He will never pass you by. He will come straight to where you are and heal you and place you in the care of a community that will help you and aid you back to health. This is why society can't come to terms with Jesus.

In all of this pain, we are taught to cover it up and hide

it and conceal it. To pretend it's not there. For men, we are taught not to cry, and for women, it's to run to the arms of the knight in shining armor. Yet the God-Man from Bethlehem comes directly to us and patches us up with grace and mercy and forgiveness while the world watches. Let there not be another day where you feel passed by and untouchable. He's inviting you on this adventure, and He needs you to bring your dream with you.

11

Lost and Loved

While we are lost, we are so loved.

Have you ever gotten lost? It may be the worst feeling on the planet. In our day and age, we have the blessing of modern technology at our dispense with GPS (Global Positioning System) and mapping systems. Could you imagine the horror of being raised in the 1800s? No sense of where you're heading; you're just heading somewhere. That's a nightmare to me. Not for the disciples, though.

They were handpicked by God to follow God (literally), but they weren't guaranteed anything but the physical presence of Jesus. At times I wonder if they felt lost as they followed this Man whom they really and truly didn't know. Yet, they still followed Him and trusted in Him while they were in lonely places.

There were moments where they weren't even allowed to enter where they used to be out of fear of retaliation against the Man they followed who had performed countless miracles at this time. All at once, they left all they knew, fishing and taxes, and went into the great unknown with Jesus.

If you're reading this and you feel you are all alone, with no one to go to, you have Jesus. He's your ever-present help in moments of trouble, and He's a friend that sticks closer than a brother. Mark my words, there will be times where all you have is Jesus, and He's the only One who will listen to you and tend to your every need while everybody else has left you or gotten caught up in their own need. He's at your next corner, and He's waiting for you at the next turn you take as you traverse this paralyzing space of misdirection.

Are you like me? I need my phone wherever I am going because, without it, I'd go missing for a solid three hours trying to find my way. It's the greatest invention of our current day in my own thought, and it's gotten me out of so many places when I did not know where I was going. Without my phone, I'd be a lost cause. Without Jesus, I shudder at the thought. Sadly though, this is the truth for many people right now.

There's a lot of people in our lives missing. Not physically, but spiritually. They have no sense of home and no

sense of belonging because they've been drifting and float-
ing for some time now. Maybe it's you. Maybe at times, it's
your spouse. We all have experienced lostness.

We can come to the honest conclusion that even when
we have accepted Jesus' plan for our lives, we at times
can still feel lost. This is called the process. We are in love
with this Man named Jesus, we pray a prayer recited by the
preacher, we commit everything to Him, and we get baptized, and then we go back to work with full knowledge of
His plan for our lives but then ten years pass and you're not
sure of where you're going, and you don't know how to get
there.

Before I worked in full-time ministry at New Life,
I landed in financial services. Don't ask me how; I just
always thought to work at a bank would be cool, but, boy,
was I wrong. If you're in banking, God be with you. It's a
unique conundrum of high customer service combed with
vehement sales. All the while keeping track of your month-
ly and daily goals.

This is where I felt lost. God takes you through these
feelings to mold you into who you're becoming though we
would love to skip the process. Here it is, though, if you
skip the process, you miss Jesus. God was teaching me

reliance and dependence in that valley season. From a very young age, I knew I wanted to help people and work within the church, and here I was, doing what I didn't want to do. I was lost, but God was showing me something that I would have missed if I had skipped over it.

He was showing me trust, He was showing me the contentment that stretched beyond my current circumstance, and He was allowing me to be humbled because when you're young, you have pride. We all do. It's what we deal with as humans. We believe we can do it on our own when in reality, we aren't doing any better. Do you want to get better? You need Him. He's your true north, as they say.

Those long days and nights at the credit union taught me that He is truly all I need, and He's all you need. Do you feel like you've lost your way? He's right where you left Him. Whether it was that traumatic experience and you blamed Him, He's waiting to be found there. We are usually trying to find God when, in all honesty, He is right where you last heard Him. For me, He was waiting to be found in the very people He was calling me to serve in that season.

When we are lost or feel lost, we miss the very thing that God has placed in front of us to serve. If you're married, you're called to serve your spouse, your kids, and your family. When you're lost, you can't see them through the discombobulation of pain, confusion, and fog. This is how affairs happen. This is how abandonment happens. The individual gets lost, and through some rather poor decision making, they are creations of their own choices.

For me, I was missing real pain and really hurting people around me while I was so caught up in the inconvenience of not being where I wanted to be. In other words, I was so selfish to my own pain and my own preference I was missing the main thing. It all changed for me in one day.

Stories

On this particular day, my time was running up, and I was only a few weeks away from resigning to go after ministry. Excitement was an understatement. This specific valley was coming swiftly to an end, and I was ready to take on the horizon and all of its challenges. Until God showed me He wasn't done with the inside of me.

Typically we experience a side to our Creator while we are lost that we otherwise would not have known while on the mountaintop. This causes us to appreciate the valley seasons while we have seemingly lost our way. Please know, God loves you while you're lost. He knows exactly where you are, and He is guiding every step of your path and your future. Is His will for you to stay lost? Of course not.

We discover that through the very story of the Israelite people while they wandered for decades until they got to where God had promised them and was leading them to. In all of His sovereignty and His plan and for us here today, we can discover through the ancient text that the people learned through this process, and they had to go through it. You're going to have to go through that trial and desert season to discover who God is, and the result will be a greater internal work that nothing else could have accomplished but that season.

The day progressed, business, as usual, until right before closing. This sweet, fragile woman came in with nothing but a warm smile, which was missing a few teeth and a slip. This is a safe place, right? I didn't want to help this lady. There were more important matters to tend to, and she was just in the way. Through the lobby and the line of clients, I could tell she would eventually be helped by yours truly.

She took her place and handed me this slip, and as I unfolded it, I realized it was a death certificate. This made the service more complicated because we had to follow a specific checklist to close accounts related to a deceased member of the financial institution. In other words, more work that I had a bad attitude about. I'm thankful God is patient with us while we give Him attitudes He was never deserving of. As the transaction continued, I retreated to the printer to retrieve an item, and that's when cold, hard conviction hit me like a hammer.

By nature, I am more inquisitive of just about everything under the sun. Curiosity hasn't killed me yet. If somebody is hurting, I like to figure out why. If there's an argument, I enjoy hearing and seeing both sides. I'm just curious, and I always had been. Upon arrival at the printer, I discovered the cause of death on this death certificate.

Suicide by gunshot. This woman whom we'll name Joan had not alerted me to the fact nor given me the slightest hint that her husband, now deceased, had taken his own life. When I took a seat back at the desk with her, everything was changed in my perspective of Joan. Joan stared warmly at me as I proceeded, but then she began telling the story of their long marriage. Joan had been married since she was eighteen; Joan was told by her husband that they would be married at that young age. Eventually, they had kids and built a life together.

Through the warmest interaction, she didn't appear at all grieved or hurt. This baffled me. How could one stay so composed while their other half just left them? So abruptly and so harshly? This is where I will always remember this story.

"He told me he would marry me when we first met," Joan stated. I nodded as she continued. "We had kids together; we loved each other; we were married for more than forty years."

What she spoke next has changed my life. You see, through this elderly woman with a few teeth missing but the warmest smile, God spoke straight to me and my situation. We all deal with shame for the things we've done. If you don't, give me what you're drinking. I've had shame. When I was only sixteen, as any young, naive teenager would be, I gave away my innocence to somebody who was not worthy of this treasure that God placed in me.

You have that story too, don't you? You were abused at a young age, and you've felt it was your fault, and you haven't told anybody. There are secrets you've been storing away, and they are currently damaging you emotionally and even, quite possibly, physically. The effects of shame and guilt go far beyond our feelings. We feel the turmoil these inflict on us from within—our deepest parts.

One of the greatest beliefs I hold is that next to the power of death, hell, and the grave that Jesus broke on the cross was His blood that beat shame and broke it. Shame doesn't have a place in your life. Those things that were done to you or you were at fault for, shame has no more power on you. You're free to live the life God has for you. You can be free from everything and everyone in your life.

Joan stared at me as I hung on every word she said and continued with these words, "I'm just so proud of him."

How can you state such scandalous words of the loved one you gave your life to, only for them to quit on you? Forever? How can you be proud of that? This is not logical, and this doesn't make sense. That's your story, and that's mine.

We made decisions that wrecked God and grieved God, and that were to our extreme detriment, and yet God still stays proud of us. Every day we are faced with two choices, to love God or to love everything else, and even after we have abandoned Him, He loves us. Even while we are lost and alone and afraid and anxious and depressed, God is after us. Deliberately after you and solely you.

The relentless and passionate pursuit of God will never truly be understood on this side of eternity, but it will be shown through His sons and daughters. Allow me to remind you, friend, that you're still His child. He's still proud of you. He's still in love with you. No sin too great and no shame too deep can conceal the burning love He has for you.

It may be time to accept it completely. This might be your salvation moment. Wherever you're reading this from, I believe God has been trying to get your attention for some time now and today is the day to give your focus to Him. He's ready to change your life from the inside out, and He's ready to introduce Himself to you as Savior, Friend, Father, Redeemer, and Healer. He introduced Himself as the Shepherd to the sheep, and that's us.

One view of Jesus we gain from the ancient Scriptures is that of a Shepherd. In Bible days, the Shepherd knew all of His sheep. No matter the size of the pasture or the quantity of the sheep. He would do whatever it took to get sheep back, too, even if it cost Him His whole life.

We all left Jesus at one point to pursue our own desires. Yet, in His grace, He pursued us through every valley and every pasture to get us back. Shepherds were faced with the worst of prey at night, yet this Shepherd was faced with the prey of all, death. Prey stared Jesus down on the cross, and we were the sheep He pursued. It cost Him everything to purchase us back.

We were lost in sin, addictions, drugs, habits, and patterns, and He still went after us. The Pharisees that put Him there on the cross were the subject of His love and affection and grace. He's the God of both, and He's on your side. God is beckoning you onward now to His way of life and His way of doing things. It's the greatest decision you'll ever make, too.

This doesn't promise you a pain-free life or a life that is free from disappointment; it just promises you won't go through life alone. He's with you to the end. He's your company while everyone else has walked away. In that empty house, after all the kids have moved out, He's there. After the death of your dearly beloved, He's there. After the divorce, He's present and near.

One attribute of God that will always be a close and intimate favorite of mine, and I know it'll bless you, is that He is present. His presence is present with you in your hardest moments. He is near to the brokenhearted, and He is ever so close to those in their most painful of times. He's shown up in the hotel room for me. He's shown up in the job interview. He's shown up in the wilderness, too.

There is confidence as I write this to you that He'll show up in your life if you haven't felt Him in a while. He has a way of showing up on time in the moments you feel as if you can't do it. He's right on schedule for you and your life, even if you feel life has passed you by. He can redeem any amount of time lost while you were lost, and He can do it in a moment. It's not too late for you, and it's not too late for His love to shine through.

12

Invisible and Invited

If you feel invisible, it's all right.

Earlier in this book, I had mentioned that there were about six or seven different elementary schools I attended. This created a lot of issues that I am currently working through now. Consistently, being the new kid created advantages but also disadvantages. God didn't create me as the most social butterfly in the class and that mixture combined with being the new kid on the block for what seemed like forever did not give me the certain aptitude to branch out. To be fully known. This would erupt as I got older.

There are moments where we truly can feel unseen by people and the world itself. In the vastness of time and space, we feel invisible and alone. For some of us, the challenge is that we have grown used to this, and now we just identify as invisible. There are plus and minus to this. A plus is people won't get to know you and your complicated life, but the minus is quite similar; people won't get to know you—your story.

Your story is what makes you unique, and we all have one. Nothing was handed to you without first being handed down by God's desk. This bears repeating, but God did not authorize the cancer or the divorce, but He did see it coming because He knows it's going to be a beautiful testimony one day. One hope I carry is that through these pages, you have discovered how to take your story and present it to God, knowing He's going to use it. Here is the catch, it can't be redeemed or revealed until it's been placed in His hands. We don't do the redeeming; God does.

Nothing takes God by surprise. Your bad days or your good days, He has seen all of them. This used to bother me, though, because I had a hard time understanding what that meant, but now I know it entirely for your story and for my own. He's aware of the days ahead so that you know who is truly handling all of it. He's inviting you in on this perspective that can aid and assist you well.

This can ease a little bit of your anxious thoughts; this can alleviate a bit of your heavy heart. You can breathe again. From the darkest night to the brightest moment, He's there, and He's close to you while you feel invisible. Here's one thing I've come to know about being invisible. God hides what is most precious to Him. He hid His Son in the tomb for three days, and the greatest gift to humanity was birthed through that miraculous event.

He hid Daniel in the den at the hands of corrupt men but not to harm him but to show the world who has the final word and final say. To feel invisible is a scary place, though, because you can really worry about if people really see you or hear you. That's twofold, to be unheard and to be out of sight. Actually, it's threefold. Out of sight, out of mind.

Do you feel invisible? It's all right. What is not okay is to stay that way. We are born for community and for friendship and relationships and to branch out and to be known by our closest friends. This is what life is all about, God and His own creation around you.

Playgrounds

Because of my predicament of being new and alone, I fell in love with reading at an early age. Dragons, wizards, and castles were my escape as everything around me seemed to be falling apart. Reading has a way of taking you out of what you are currently residing in. Now imagine the power the biblical narrative has while you're going through hell. It can take you into hope while hopelessness is all around. It can take you into strength while you're feeling weakness and weariness all around. It's supernatural for a reason.

The most hated and attacked book in history, yet we can't contain it, and we can't cancel it. People literally thought Jesus didn't rise again on the third day; they thought His own disciples hid His body with the fairytale that He rose again to inspire an insurrection among those who believed He was who He said He was. Yet, Jesus did rise again, and because of that, I know I don't have to stay invisible any longer.

With no friends to run to or to play with, recess was the worst nightmare for me at school. I did what I always did, book in hand and a cozy bench at my disposal. For the whole block of time, while I should have been doing what the other kids were doing, I was captivated by the words on the page. At a certain point, you just get used to feeling the way you're feeling.

Please hear me, you've been feeling depressed for quite some time, and now you're used to it. You've been feeling hurt for a long time, and now you're used to it. God is about transformation and change (He Himself doesn't change), and He's about to change you from the inside out. He's that God. He changed the murderer in the prison cell, and He changed the drug-addicted mom. He can change you.

Up until one day, everything changed. I was invisible; I felt it and lived it until I was invited to play. All it took was another friend whom I love to this day to extend an open invitation to go play with him and the others in his class. I don't think I picked up a book at recess from then on. It all shifted.

God has invited you already to His life-transforming power; the tension is in the question will we accept the offer? What's waiting for you on the other side is greater than anything you could ever imagine or think of: a land full of blessing, grace, and mercy. All of which doesn't run out. He's beckoning you to this life filled with pain, grief, hardship, love, fun, and family.

What often can happen is while we feel invisible, we feel alone. This is where the community comes into a greater play in your life. You need community. You need a local body of believers around you who can help you and show you their own story while you go and grow through your own. It's so crucial.

We read and believe the words that God wrote to us

that it really is not beneficial to be alone. Yet, here we are, forced into isolation during this worldwide phenomenon taking place before our eyes. Isolation is the new normal, it seems. Looking around, though, we can tell the extreme detriment this is to us as humans.

People are angrier, more anxious, more down and out. The evidence is all around that loneliness is a breeding ground for lostness, hopelessness, and invisibility. This does not have to be your story either. It's going to take courage and an extra fifteen or twenty-minute drive in your week to extend past your comfort zone and get into a church. The church has never been more alive and ready to welcome you and your problems with open arms. You see, the church exists for broken people like you and me to come together to glorify One man who fixes our broken state.

Now, this is worth the mention, but the church, the one Jesus died for, is not perfect. It's filled with imperfect people to speak about a perfect God. Anytime people are involved, mistakes will happen and hurts will occur. You're going to be hurt and affected by it, but that is not your moment to retreat. It's an invitation to press in and keep believing in the people God has placed in your life. We often give up on the most beneficial needs we have in front of us, and this isn't the time to give in but to hang in there. Heartaches will happen, and disappointments will happen, but I'd rather face those in a community than be invisible for the rest of my life.

What can we do in all of this? We can seek out those in our very own community who feel invisible, and we can love them right where they are at. Nobody else is seeking them out. Nobody else even really cares, but as people who follow Jesus, we seek, and we go after, and we press into them, and we love them with the same love that He lavished on us. Practically what does this look like?

We invite the broken and single parent to a small group or connect group. You send the text to that family and encourage them that you'll see them this weekend at your worship experience. The addicted college guy or gal is waiting on you to see if you really care. That's what we are all really after, anyway. Do we care enough to pull the veil back from their eyes and show them they don't have to stay invisible any longer?

Waiting

The most crucial and painful times of being invisible can be those moments where you feel as if you're waiting on the plan and promise of God for your life. Remember, it's in the "and." God is the God of both, the waiting and the walking into what He has for you. In this context, though, I mean waiting tables. Straight out of high school, I waited tables. This was an exhilarating career change for me from the grocery store. Let's be honest, I was ready to make more money, too.

On this particular night, it might have been a Team Night at the high school down the way; it was chaos. Every table in this establishment was filled, and I was overwhelmed. While I waited, I was buckling under the stress and tension of the needs around me. Do you know what I mean? The kids need your attention, the spouse needs your attention, and now your job is begging for better performance.

This reality is true for many of us. We are buckling under the pressure of the day-to-day needs around us while forgetting to take care of ourselves, and we drift slowly towards the invisible backdrop. At this moment, I was buckling under the needs of the tables around me, and one patron noticed. At his call, I proceeded to the table, expecting a lesson to be taught or a complaint to be had. It was neither.

The invitation was for me to be seated. To take a seat at the table I was waiting on. This amazing patron called me out of the chaos and invited me to take a seat at his table with him and his guests, and to this day, I cannot tell you what he said, but I can remember how he made me feel. He made me feel seen, and he validated my emotions to what was happening around me. We have this opportunity all around us to invite people to where we are seated and show them that we see them, that we hear them.

We really can save lives by this. We really can make a difference at this moment, and this day we live in by stopping to pause in a rushed world and extend the opportunity for those around us who feel invisible to be loved and accepted as they are. Jesus was really good at seeking those who society had cast out, and He made them known, loved, and valued. Above all? He healed them. We have that same opportunity extended to us, and He's with us every step of the way as we invite the invisible or as we step out of being unseen.

13

Mess and Miracle

The mess is a prerequisite to the miracle.

Before we continue on in this chapter, I wanted to take a moment and personally let you know that some stories do not end in a happy ending. One of the greatest mysteries to me is the thought that He has all the authority in heaven and on earth, yet He allows an ending to be sad and, at times, even tragic. Life really does have an unfortunate way of bringing about messes, trials, and tragedies.

There's unspeakable pain in just about every day we wake up now. It's our normal. We've been at times desensitized to the trauma around us that we cannot even begin to process the personal trauma we have internally. Thank God we have a Counselor who knows our pain and our struggles, and He knows when He needs to be our Counselor instead of our Champion.

We make messes of just about everything we touch, don't we? We mess up marriages, we mess up jobs, we mess up friendships, and we mess up ourselves. It's our curse, unfortunately. Humans have been messing with God's plan since the beginning of time. This has been shown to us by the world we live in and inhabit today. Sadly, the greatest messes we see are usually caused by those closest to us.

Jamie was really good at creating messes, and he had fun doing it, too. Through our childhood, we had a great relationship. We'd fight as brothers do, wrestle, yell and laugh together. We had some of the greatest conversations on car rides together. There was a season we owned this gas-guzzling SUV that was never full-on gas, and it was guaranteed Jamie would leave it on empty for me as I wanted to go out with no money.

Do you feel empty? All the time? Never full? Life has a unique way of doing that to us. We are confronted with circumstances and relationships that are beyond our control at times, and we are left empty like that SUV. This may be why you feel so weak and so tired because you're so empty. There are some spaces that only Jesus can fill.

Drugs cannot fill that space for you; porn cannot fill that hole for you; food cannot satisfy that innate craving within your own soul. Yet, we pursue these items all the time. This is to our extreme detriment, and it's at the expense of our very own pain and the pain of our close loved ones. We turn to faulty and frail objects and desires that we think will satisfy our hurts and heartaches. This is our problem.

Will God come to our rescue? Of course. Will God forgive us for our ridiculous patterns and ways? Absolutely. Yet, this does not mean He can help us with the consequences of our actions. He cannot stop the jail time if you are, in fact, guilty as charged. When Adam and Eve did what they did, it bore a consequence for humanity.

Our decisions will either better us or hurt us, and in the end, we are the ones that truly ruined ourselves. Not God. Not others. Our own mistakes. Yet, this is where the beauty is in all of it; God can redeem even the worst of mistakes and decisions. He's done it before, and He will do it time and time again.

Decisions

Jamie knew how to make decisions, and indecision was never in his vocabulary or everyday exercises. If he wanted something, he would go get it. At a young age, he recruited me to work a lawn mowing business in the neighborhood; the only caveat was that he was the owner, and I happened to be the only employee. We were respectively only about twelve and thirteen if my memory serves me properly.

Why? Because he wanted money for the newest gadget or shoes. He was a tremendous businessman at a young age. He made up his mind, and nothing was too far out of his reach to attain. Unfortunately, this did not translate to his academics. He was honestly the worst student the school had, but the teachers loved him. People loved him.

He was on everybody's contact list, and he was at every gathering there was to be had. He had the social bend that I never got. He was great at making friends and making memories. Unfortunately, some friends are never made for making. In your life and my own. We must be cautious about who we allow in our lives. They'll either serve God's purpose for your life or serve an entirely opposite one. Paul even lets us in on a secret that explains to us that we become like who we are around.

This is how the devil works, you know. Yes, I do believe in evil, but we give him too much airtime in the media today, and this is his only spot. At the very end of the narrative. Thank God that he didn't get the last word in this story, and we'll live every day making him pay. His influence is to the destruction of every human on the planet, and he is at play in our decisions.

It's a devious way of doing business, too, because it's subtle. Satan loves the subtle because he knows if he can get one bad decision, you'll slowly erode and make more bad decisions until it's too late and you are at the end of your rope. For those reading this and you feel at the end of your own rope, it's not too late. You can still live, you can still fight forward, you can still move on. All it takes is one moment of acknowledgment to God our Father, and He can redeem a whole life's worth of mistakes and tragedies.

Jamie allowed the wrong influences in his life, and first, honestly, it was hilarious. He got caught once for sneaking out, and the police gladly escorted him back home to be greeted by the belt. He had a way of continuing on, though, even in the face of discipline. One thing we know, though, God disciplines those He loves. He loves you, and He disciplines you to keep you on track and on pace with His plan for your life.

Don't reject the discipline; that would be to your detriment and heartache. Discipline helps you grow into who you're becoming. It's the bridge between where you are now and who you're growing into becoming. It might hurt (literally), and it may be uncomfortable at the time, but it's all worth it in the end. He's taking you somewhere with it and through it all.

For those who have had the privilege of having siblings, you know the joy there is in it all. They are there for you on every holiday, road trip, and birthday. They teach you a lot about your family and yourself, for that matter. At the end of the day, the minor annoyance that can be provided by them is really momentary.

Jamie and I used to beat each other after school. Not in a race, we'd beat our bodies in improvised wrestling matches. We'd usually start pretty civil until he started to antagonize further and further, and I'd go in for the kill. That's what siblings do. No matter the elevated state of affairs, you're always in love with one another and there for each other.

Our culture today speaks the exact opposite of that. An argument arises, and we can't see the others' response or answer as valid, so we just excommunicate one another all the time. Or we just block them from our lives on social media. Our curse is our offense. I'm thankful that Jesus didn't block me when I was at my lowest. He didn't block you, either.

The cross He hung on was the greatest unblocking moment in all of humanity. From then until now and until we leap into all the future has for us. He cleared the way from us to Him, and we can live free from shame, free from people-pleasing, free from pain and guilt. He provided a way, the only way.

When the argument and matter of sin arose, He didn't step away and tell us all off; He went after us. In a relentless pursuit, He went to the darkest of places to get us back. What dark places have you been to that you have convinced He isn't there? Can I remind you He traversed the valley of hell for three days to get the keys back from death, hell, and the grave? There is no place He won't go to get back His creation.

Are you knee-deep in debt? He's going to provide a way to pay off the bills. He'll show you wisdom and how to use your finances. Are you scared of the future? He knows the great plans that He has for you, even when you don't. We can take heart in the Master of the universe who spoke it all into being.

There has been horror, rage, disease, and death all around us in this particular season we are residing in. Yet, through it all, He knows how it all ends, and He knows your name. We even know and believe that He has every hair on your head numbered. That speaks of proximity. That speaks of nearness. God is so close to you at this moment.

We get so busy we miss Him, but He's there. Whenever you're ready to acknowledge His presence and love and forgiveness, He's there to show up. I'm just going to put it out there, but the trauma you just experienced is a great prerequisite to His presence in your life. It creates an atmosphere where His love breaks through and permeates into your life, and you can't help but realize He's alive and real.

To the one struggling with the belief in a living and breathing God, you can be assured today that He's aware of you. He's involved in your life more than you think He is. God is in the backdrop of your life, working behind the scenes. Your struggle and doubt don't have to be the end of the story; God's love can be. His Person can be.

He's the only one that is possible in all of this impossible hardship we are dealing with. His love is possible. His grace is attainable. His mercy is ever with us. His attributes outnumber the stars in the sky, and He's obsessed with you. We don't need a quarter in a candy machine to access this gum; we just need the faith to spin the gadget and believe it's already been paid for.

December

My dad, like any parent, had a hard time with the drug abuse from his own son, so he did what he thought was the greatest thing to do, evicted my brother from his bedroom, and had him figure it out. Sadly, over time, we just grew apart. Jamie was around for Sunday afternoon lunches and hangouts but as the time drifted, so did his mind to the constant abuse of his actions. He wasn't truly the same. He was still funny, charismatic, and sharp but underneath was an underlying issue of deterioration.

Senior year was going as well as it could be going. The nights consisted of energy drinks and video games, honestly. The fall semester went by fast, and Christmas break was upon us and the best news? Jamie came home. He hadn't been home for a few years and seasons since he initially departed. He and my dad made amends, and he was allowed to be home with us.

We started off high, too. Not literally. We went to the gym together, which is something we did together in earlier years of our lives. It was awesome to have my older brother back home. Things felt normal after a period of not feeling so.

On a Wednesday night, dad, Jamie, and I decided to go to the weekly church gathering at the church we grew up in. You have to understand, we hadn't been to church together in a long time, so this was a miracle in itself. We made it up the long parking lot, found our way to our seats, and the worship started. This was and still is today an incredible church. I credit it to my dad for allowing us to grow up there, and a lot of my faith was subtly developed in this house.

If you're in church at all, you know what an altar call is. In this instance, though, Jamie wasn't following particular church protocol. He persisted to the altar a dozen times before the first song even concluded. At that time, it was honestly rather annoying up until this moment.

There are moments that you never forget; this is one of them for me. In the battle with drugs, Jamie's frame had shrunken a bit, and he had gotten skinny. To see this skinny brother of mine lean over into my dad's broad shoulder and whisper something that is more valuable than gold or silver.

"Dad, I'm saved," Jamie whispered in an innocent, childlike manner.

Precious is an understatement. The beauty in it? Incomparable. My brother, who had dealt with his fair share of heartache and pain, had met and encountered the love of the Father at this moment. It was a sight to behold, and the words haven't left my memory since.

We celebrated at the local waffle place, and we laughed, we talked, we hung out together as father and sons came together. This was our moment, and nothing was taking it from us. There was beauty in this cold night in Georgia. The best ahead looked promising.

In your life and in my own, we need to take a look at the future with expectation and anticipation that God is going to do some incredible things through our lives; that He is going to move in a mighty way on our behalf. We are His kids, after all. We cannot allow life to hurt us and get us to the place of pain and remorse where we stop looking ahead. That isn't faith. Faith is the belief that there is still good ahead if you have only been faced with pain. Some dreams and inspirations cannot be brought back to life, though.

The next few weeks felt like a dream, if we are being honest. Family dinners happened again. Movie nights happened again. Jamie smoked cigarettes, so there was that, too. Unfortunately for Jamie, his drug abuse persisted, too. This is for every believer or non-believer that Jesus, at times, is not an instant cure for our pain.

Yes, He forgives us and helps us in our pain, but sometimes addiction doesn't leave after we say our prayer and commit our lives to Him. As a matter of fact, it might even get worse for you after that prayer has been said and you have said you would follow Him all the days of your life. Not to get very theologically in-depth, but this is something called sanctification.

Simply, it means you are becoming like Him as each day passes. We still have parts of us that we do not appreciate, and that's where His grace comes into play each and every day of our lives. That's where our dependence on Him gets greater and greater. We really won't be perfected until we get to our home with Jesus.

Resuscitation

Christmas was the best (they always were), and we were coming off the heels of the beauty of being together again. We all went out the next day with our friends and celebrated with them over the festivities and food. I had pulled into the driveway late at night, and everybody was home, but something was off.

Jamie was at the table, food in hand, but he was experiencing the effects of whatever he had partaken of just hours before this. He came home messed up before, but not like this. He was out of his mind, and he was barely there. As every other time had passed before our eyes, an argument was had over it, and I ended up tucking him into bed.

He slept on our couch in the upstairs loft we had. His eyes glazed over by the evil inside; he looked tired. Lying him down to sleep, turning off the TV, and heading to bed myself, I was looking forward to the gym the next day. Selfish.

Waking up, I put on my gym clothes and went to the gym. I grew up in and out of the gym; it was and still is my God-given therapy. We all need something healthy to turn to while the world tries to feed us items that are unnecessary to our health and wellbeing. The workout went great, and the brisk, cold December air bit me as I drove home and went into the shower.

As fast as I could turn on the water, I heard a scream that would make any spine tingle. In my rushed state, I ended up in the loft of our home where Jamie had just been lain to sleep the night previous. Only Jamie wasn't breathing. He was cold.

We were lifeguards together, and those memories and impulses came back quickly as my dad and I did what anybody would do: we tried to put life back into his body. Performing life-saving measures doesn't really work well on the couch, so I cradled his cold and skinny frame in my arms and placed him delicately on the carpet. Father and son, side by side, doing what we could do. Compression after compression. All of my strength poured into my arms as I did what I could, and my dad did what he could to bring Jamie back to the land of the living. Seconds turned into minutes, and minutes turned into doubt, and doubt turned into panic.

Nothing was happening. There wasn't anything happening. In all the movies, it seemed so easy. Here in this moment, it felt as if there was ever even a window; it was closing and closing rapidly. The paramedics were called, and we kept compressing. We kept breathing.

All those memories, all those life experiences, all those times at the swimming pool, all those movie dates, everything came to the forefront of my memory as we did what we could to breathe life into Jamie as the disease of addiction had overtaken him and stolen the promise of his future. The evil behind the drug abuse was too strong at this moment for our feeble hands and attempts. Jamie was gone.

How can we go from one week together, enjoying all that life has to offer to this? Some stories don't end the way we wish that they would. There isn't an alternate ending here. The coroner had explained to us thereafter that the powerful concoction of drugs Jamie had taken was enough to stop his heart throughout the night. The painful question remains for us here, where is the miracle in all of this?

Death

Nobody can prepare you for the journey that grief is. Grief is truly unexplainable in words, and it's poignant in our present-day circumstances. King David wrote to us out of an ancient psalm, and he was on to something (I mean it is the Bible) when he put it into words what it would be like to walk through the darkest valley of death. Let's be honest, those that have passed are gone, and in most cases, if they were a believer in Jesus, we believe they are in the arms of the great Healer. For us? We are here left to navigate the pain, confusion, and heartache.

The miracle is in the valley, though. Through this Psalm, we are shown that God is truly with us and at our side. In my belief and conviction, God is who He says He is, and He makes Himself known in our grief. Finality is one of the hardest things we can deal with, knowing it's finished. No more conversations. No more car rides. None of that. What is left, though?

Our miracle-making God. He still makes miracles happen, and He still is writing our story. Through the abuse, bad choices, and heartaches, He is in control, and He is faithful to complete everything He started in you. You see, death may be the end for our loved ones, but it's the start of something brand new for us still here.

14

Grief and Grace

There's a grace for you in every season.

We drove to the hospital swiftly after the paramedics picked up Jamie. There was still some hope in us that they could provide and administer a life-saving drug that was more powerful than my own two hands and my own effort. In my own life, I've been blessed with the outlook of hope, even in the darkest of circumstances. There's still hope for you. As long as Jesus is on the scene, there will always be hope for humanity. When Jesus shows up, He changes things. Situations shift. Seasons go, and storms end.

This is what Jesus does, but the hard and sobering question remains, what if He doesn't do it? What if He doesn't save the life? What if He doesn't heal the cancer? We praise Him anyways. We choose Him still. He's our only shot at this life.

He's the only hope for the addict, for the high school jock, for the struggling businessman, and for you. We only have access to One true light in this dark and diseased world, and that's Jesus. Jesus is the hope of the world, and we have the greatest message to tell. This is why the disciples did what they had to do after Jesus ascended to heaven. They had news to spread, and we do, too.

In a world full of bad news and fearful rhetoric, we can be the ones who share the hope of all humanity. We can be the people that refuse to believe in the fear and choose to believe in faith that Jesus is working and with us in these chaotic moments. This is the hour that is critical to us, where we stop listening to the panic, and we start to fill our vocabulary with praise to the One who has this whole scenario in His hands.

We rolled up into the hospital and were escorted into the lobby and placed in a private room. We waited there for moments, and the grief was gripping us. We all believed there was still some hope. There in the room, we had no words; we just had each other. All we've got in this life is each other.

Why do we allow offenses and division to separate us? We are never stronger than when we are together. More battles are won when we spend them together, fighting as one, united and not divided. That's the Gospel, and that's our hope. We allow grief to split families down the middle. Funerals are a great revealer of the internal conditions of families and extended relationships on both sides. There's no blame on anybody; it's just what grief does.

There was a slight knock on the door, and the doctor came in. In the most caring and professional way possible, he had explained that they had truly done everything in their power to revive Jamie, but none of it was able to restart his heart. Silence was thick as it was followed by sorrow in all of us. We were all feeling this pain.

What has given me hope about this story is that God wrote it. He allowed it to happen, but it was to breed something out of all of it. In the next moment, none of us were ready for the request. We were welcomed by the local authorities, and they needed an account of the last twenty-four hours of Jamie's life. We were still processing the grief of the moment, and they wanted a story.

At that moment, I stood for the occasion and walked back into a labyrinth of deeper hallways—just me. I followed them as they led me into a room and behind a curtain, and there Jamie laid. He looked at rest for the first time in a rough few years. He was truly at peace. The authorities present proceeded to ask me questions in regards to his whereabouts and who he could have possibly been with. For me, it was one last moment with Jamie, and the pain of it all was more than I could bear.

There is a specific grace for you and in your season right now. God has given you all you need to deal with every issue in your life right now. Every trial. He's more than present with you and your pain. What we often fail to do is acknowledge God at the moment. We fall short of including Him in our struggles at the workplace. We forget to place Him where He rightfully belongs to be, in the middle of our trouble.

I can't remember the questions they asked me; I can only see Jamie. Yet in rearview, God was so present there in that space, and I wish I had acknowledged Him at that moment. The whole season of grief that followed was filled with rage and hurt. I was mad at God and mad at the world. Nothing really prepares you for death and the aftermath. But God is so patient and so kind.

Aftermath

For the next few months, there was little acknowledgment to the God who made me and formed you. Anger, grief, and sadness were all evident. Yet God gives us space to wrestle and to learn. God doesn't leave us nor forsake us; we believe that. God somehow, in all His power, still creates an atmosphere that He's present yet gives us a place to process our pain. This is where most Christians leave the faith.

Most Sunday's we were forcefully dragged to church. Week after week, we filled the seats in that auditorium where Jamie, Dad, and I had visited before his death. To say the least, I was rooted in the faith, and this present circumstance pulled me out of everything I was raised in. Circumstances have a way of doing that. This was a season of doing whatever I wanted without the acknowledgment of God in my life. Yet, God was always there. He is still here.

There is no aftermath that He can't help with in your life. We are dealing on the daily with the aftermath of many choices and decisions and actions in our lives, and God is still ever-present and ready to help us with the ripples. He'll help you through people; He'll help you through it all.

It was a surreal moment for me as I returned to school after winter break. Senior year is supposed to be filled with expectation and anticipation of all that is to come as we enter adulthood, but this was filled with despair and grief. There wasn't any other will but my own. To be candid, I didn't have the will to finish my classes but thank God for teachers who pushed you in the right direction.

They were patient, kind, and considerate as news of my brother's passing spread through the hallways of the school. In every way possible, they helped me finish and graduate when all I wanted to do was leave it all behind. Anger, disbelief, disorientation, and pain were all I could see and feel. The valley of shadow of death was painful, and it still is. This, though, isn't an excuse to leave the faith.

We leave because we are angry. We leave because we are hurt. We leave because we are troubled and imperfect, yet we forget that the presence of God is our place to process those emotions. He can handle the emotions that He created and placed in you. Your emotions are great signals to what He is trying to help you with.

Do you know how many people have left marriages out of anger? Churches out of offense? Employers out of inconvenience? We get angry and bitter and filled with resentment all the time because we haven't forgotten the ancient practice of just bringing the matter to God and His hands. He has all you need to process those emotions deep down.

Thank God I didn't stay angry. You don't have to either. God is waiting on the other side of all that anger and rage to let you know that He sees you, and He's with you through all of it. He loved me at my worst when I was the farthest away from Him, and He still welcomed me back into His arms. He still offered me a spot at His table. There's one for you, too.

Feelings

It's a valid question to ask of us right now as we approach the end of this journey together. What're your feelings telling you? What're they showing you? We all have emotions, and we all have trouble processing them at times. Just ask the poor barista at the local coffee shop. They have seen the worst of human emotion.

Your feelings should not deter your faith. Faith is not a formula or a feeling, it's an action, and it's a person. We believe in Jesus despite all the pain we have felt. We believe in Jesus despite the inconvenience. Let's be candid; what's the alternative? Do we grow and get bitter?

Nobody wakes up in the morning wishing we would get bitter. Our emotions can help us get better. They aid our existence here on planet Earth. They enrich our relationships. They add flavor to a flavorless world. They add color to a black and white existence.

Your feelings don't determine your destiny, but they sure can drive you to the destination of your choice if you allow them to. In my own story, after months of rejecting the God of the universe, He slowly started to peel back the layers of my feelings.

Slowly but surely, He was crafting a passion inside of me through this modern-day hell. He's crafting a passion through your pain, too. Passion is developed from pain, and you know what I can say before you today? God is good. He's present, and He's available, and He's aware of you and your situation.

What gives me hope today is that there isn't anything I would change about my story, though I would love to. Yet, He's the God of both sides. He's been on both sides of the tomb. He's seen your life on both sides, from birth to the cemetery. He's seen the hard times, and He's seen the bad times. He has been with you in the valleys, and He has been with you in the highs.

God was there when my brother wouldn't come back to life, and God was there when we said our final goodbyes at the funeral. This fuels my feelings. It doesn't make me bitter; it makes me better. It should fuel your gratitude, too, and it should breed confidence in your life right now.

The decision is ours now. Will we allow our life's experiences to hinder our faith or enhance it? We have to choose because, as we have discovered, it's never been "or." It's "and." He's the God of the good and the bad. The hard and the soft. The broken, blessed, limping, and cheering.

He's your God, too. My prayer is that this small journey we have taken together, this slight glimpse into my life and all its pain, triumph, and love, is a testimony to the grace of God, and it can be your story too. You see, the same grace that is available to me today is available for you, too. Our stories may look completely different, but we have the same God who is familiar with you. He knows what you're going through, and you do not have to do it alone.

What's the alternative? Do we try to do it all on our own? Good luck with that. At this moment, the choice is yours. Acknowledge your need for a Savior who loves you so much that He gave Himself for you and His free gift of forgiveness. On the other side of forgiveness? A love like you have never known and a grace available to you that is for you and with you. You see, Jesus is grace personified.

He goes with you. He is for you. No weapon or bad day formed against you will prosper. He has more for you than the world has to offer, and He's waiting on you at this moment to come home and spend the rest of this life with Him. He'll take you to places you cannot even begin to imagine. He'll provide friends you didn't even know you needed. He'll comfort you, guide you, lead you, protect you, restore you and redeem you. There isn't anything He can't do, and if He did it with my story, He'd surely do it in yours, too.

Ending

If you made it this far, I pray you have picked up something of value to your life. Life is filled with deep crevices that sometimes we wish didn't exist, and it is also filled with great heights, waiting to be traversed. The truth is we can't allow either to stop our relationship with God and with people. God is the purpose you have been waiting for in this life, and people are the plan and point to this all.

This book was created and curated with you in mind through the lenses of some of my experiences here on this planet so far, and my hope is that you will put into practice something you learned throughout this journey. More than that, everything I've been given and blessed with is from Jesus, and I pray you get to know Him more and more. He's the only chance we have. He brings unity to a divided world. He brings peace to chaos and stillness to the storms.

He is the Ancient of Days; He is everything that was promised to us. His words will last through eternity, and His power will permeate through all of our lives. He'll be here long after we are gone, and He's been here before we ever were. The Gospel will never wear and tear on us; its relevance surpasses all that we know here and today. It's the only hope we have. There's a lot He can do with a life lain down, and He's waiting on you to make that decision.

Through the early mornings and late nights of this book, I really had a hard time ending it, but there's more to come from the conclusion of these pages, for you and for me. Don't drop the dream He put inside of you, don't stop loving people for who they are and not who they should be. Don't forget to love yourself and to love your neighbor. There's a lot of anger, rage, and hostility in the air, and we cannot be defined by that. We cannot let the ugly outside of us overtake the beauty within us. Don't let the hate drive your narrative; let love tell the final chapter of your life.

Epilogue

What now?

We'll make this brief, but if you just began the journey of following the Jesus I know, or you recommitted your life to Him, your next step is simple. Find a local community. Get plugged into relationships that will better you and your soul. Begin to serve somebody you know. Make the decision to get baptized. When the bad seasons come? You know fully well at this point that God is near, and there isn't a day or season He doesn't have full view of.

I hope you know that you're more loved than you know, and there's a lot of people out there who are proud of you for who you are. Let's go love people with the same love that the Father has lavished on us. We aren't wasting another day of our lives. We have a kingdom to build, and it takes your role and your position to help build it. The best is ahead of us, and the *God of Both* is on our side.

About the Author

Landon is a passionate speaker, preacher, author, and a friend to anybody he meets. He resides in Ventura, California. He and his wife, Jackie, have two daughters, Charlotte and Mila. He serves on staff at New Life Community Church in Oxnard, California. In his free time, he enjoys traveling, exercise, caffeine and cold brew, movies, and quiet time with his family and friends. You can follow him on social media and on his website.